FLIRTING WITH UNIVERSALISM

FLIRTING WITH UNIVERSALISM

Resolving the Problem of an Eternal Hell

Dennis Jensen

RESOURCE *Publications* · Eugene, Oregon

FLIRTING WITH UNIVERSALISM
Resolving the Problem of an Eternal Hell

Resource Publications
An Imprint of Wipf and Stock Publishers
199 W. 8th Ave., Suite 3
Eugene, OR 97401

www.wipfandstock.com

ISBN 13: 978-1-62564-754-2

Manufactured in the U.S.A.   05/12/2014

To George MacDonald

Will not the Judge of all the earth do right?

—GENESIS 18:25

CONTENTS

ACKNOWLEDGMENTS

My thanks to Justin and Clark Jensen for their critiques, suggestions, and time consuming analysis of this work; to Lisa Gunther, for her insights concerning an early draft of the study; to Thomas Talbott, I. Howard Marshall, and David Instone-Brewer, who, though they did not know that I was working on this book, took the time to correspond, discuss arguments, and provide insights which helped me to deal with some of the crucial issues of this text.

INTRODUCTION

Many Christians and non-Christians consider the doctrinal problem of an eternal hell, in the traditional understanding of the terms, as the greatest problem facing Christianity. Philosopher Michael Tooley says Christianity (with this teaching) is "too horrible to be true." To speak of God's love for humanity as unimaginably great and then to speak of God damning those who reject God with pain that is so horrible that it would only befit an omnipotent, psychopathic torturer who infinitely hates one's victims, is simply self-contradictory. It appears to many to be just a crude ploy thought up by heartless theologians and dogmatists. They're Jekyll and Hydes who first try to attract unbelievers by appealing to God's love and compassion but then they change into raging monsters seeking to frighten the unresponsive to convert.

John Stuart Mill, the famous philosopher and son of another great intellect, James Mill, recounted in his *Autobiography* how his father complained about Christians who hold this doctrine. He thought any god who would create such an abode of eternal torment could not possibly be considered good and that Christians who honor and emulate such a god would be inconsistent in any good that they might do. How can one obey the commands to do good of a god who does such horrendous evil?[1]

Of course, even if belief in the traditionalist hell is thought to be too evil and horrible to be true, this does not show that it

1. Mill, *Autobiography*, 28–30.

is false. It may be true and the state of the world is much worse than one would imagine. Truth and falsity must be determined by reason and evidence, not by wanting the world to be a certain way. Even if Baudelaire was right that God, and particularly the Christian God, would actually be the devil, that does not mean that there is no such devil. So if the doctrine of an eternal hell is the greatest problem for Christianity, it is not strictly an intellectual problem in the sense of providing evidence against belief; rather, it is an existential and moral problem that questions whether one should embrace Christianity even if it were known to be true.

The truth or falsity of the existence of a traditionalist hell must be determined by evidence. In exploring this evidence this study will first assume the historical evidence for Christianity.[2] This includes evidence that Jesus is the Jewish Messiah, that all that he taught is true, and that he taught that the Hebrew Scripture and the teachings of his direct disciples were and would be true. We will also assume that we have in most of the New Testament (NT) an accurate account or an adequate paraphrase of Jesus and his first apostles' teachings.[3] What we will instead need to evaluate is the evidence that he and his disciples did or did not teach this particular doctrine. We will also need to look at some philosophical arguments and problems with this belief and several alternate views of hell.

This is written for both Christians and non-Christians. Non-Christians will be interested in looking at the biblical and philosophical arguments discussed here to see whether the problem of hell can honestly be resolved. I will claim that one may embrace a deeply biblical Christianity and fully accept the goodness, love, and justice of the biblical God. I hope that Christians will see that a close examination of the Scripture does not allow for the traditional view of horrific, undiminishing torment in an eternal hell. But neither does it allow for any form of universalism which

2 To look at this evidence one might want to start with Craig, *Reasonable Faith* and Habermas and Licona, *Case for the Resurrection*.

3. See for example, Blomberg, *Historical Reliability of the Gospels*; Bruce, *New Testament Documents*.

trivializes one's obligations to God or denies God's justice. Christians also need to see that the most agonizing problem they will ever face, the problem of lost loved ones, does have an answer. I hope Christians will also be able to use this material to respond to the accusations of non-Christian critics. We must all come to see that even the most difficult and troubling theological problems have soundly biblical answers.

Before looking at what the Bible says about the afterlife of the lost, we should consider some terms I will be using. The *lost* are all those who are in some way rejected by and morally alienated from God. *Traditionalists* are those who believe the lost will endure unending, never diminishing suffering. Traditionally this suffering has been depicted as horrific suffering, though modern advocates sometimes vacillate when relating just how horrible it is. Some speak as though it isn't quite so bad after all when it is objected that this is unjust of God or that this suffering would be undeserved. Some advocates will emphasize that it is indeed *very* horrific should Christianity not be taken seriously enough. Traditionalism is the dominant, orthodox Christian view. Because traditionalism seems to me to be such an inappropriate term to describe this doctrine, hereafter I will use the term *eternalism* instead. Though still not perfect, eternalism is a much more intuitively fitting term for this view. (See figure 1 in the appendix.)

Technically, *Christian annihilationism* and *conditional immortality* (the latter is often shortened to *conditionalism*) are slightly different, though for our purposes we can use the terms interchangeably. Since some passages of Scripture I will mention indicate fairly clearly a postmortem time of suffering for the lost, Christian annihilationists typically believe God consigns the lost to a period of punishment and then brings about extinction of consciousness. Sadly, eternalist (traditionalist) critics sometimes overlook this point claiming that annihilationism fails to justly punish the lost and that it is no different than secular annihilationism.[4] The normal secular view that life ends at death we may call

---

4. See John Walvoord's eternalist critique, "Response to Clark H. Pinnock," in Crockett, *Four Views on Hell*, 168–69.

secular annihilationism. Christian annihilationism and conditionalism I will hereafter simply call annihilationism unless the context requires otherwise. (See figure 2.) Some other special terms
will be defined or explained later in this study.

The Christian has the unavoidable task of demonstrating that
the God of the Bible is not the devil or at least that the claim has
no substance. I will attempt to offer a way out of this problem by
arguing for a position between eternalism and *universalism*, universalism being the belief that all will be welcomed into paradise.
A *restorationist* form of universalism (or *restorationism*) says that
all will be saved, though, for many of the lost, only after much
suffering and purging. In my view even restorationism is unac-
ceptable because it does violence to human freedom and is less
likely biblically justified. On the other hand, I will maintain that
eternalism or traditionalism does violence to the biblical doctrine
of God's infinite love, goodness, and justice.

I would argue that a Christian annihilationist view would
adequately answer Mill's accusation. It has sufficient biblical justification to be embraced by any who accept the most basic and clear
teachings of the Bible. But there is another problem that needs to
be answered as well which makes even annihilationism inadequate
in my thinking: the problem of lost loved ones and the infinite love
of God. Let me emphasize that nothing worse than annihilationism is acceptable; annihilationism *is* the worst case scenario. But
a better answer will be found somewhere between annhilationism
and universalism.

I will first argue for two positions I would call *modified
eternalism* and *semi-restorationism*. The former view says that
the unredeemably lost will, following a time of suffering that ac-
cords with the evil they have committed, leave this painful state.
The unredeemably lost are those who, after responding negatively
to God's offer of reconciliation however many times God might
determine, will no longer be allowed the possibility of salvation.
Following the time of punishment will be a minimal, pleasureless
existence.

The latter position, semi-restorationism, some might be tempted to depict as universalism with second-class citizenship. More accurately but briefly, it says that those in the above painless/pleasureless state will then be given one enjoyment or pleasure: the joy of eternally experiencing God's love and the love of the redeemed as well as the joy of loving God and loving the redeemed. (SR in figure 3.) However, their existence will be more limited than that of the redeemed and they will forever carry the shame of having rejected their Source and Creator. It now may be evident why this study is entitled "Flirting with Universalism."

If you should find my case for semi-restorationism wanting, I would hope you see the strength of the Christian annihilationist arguments and, at the very least, not fall back on an eternalist view. Above all else, eternalism must be rejected as a Christian option.

Secondly, I will argue for a form of Christian *inclusivism* that I would call *limited potential restorationism*. Inclusivism says that one may be accepted by God, *saved* if you will, without expressing faith in Jesus Christ in this life. Some forms maintain that it is because of Christ's atoning work that one is saved, not because of one's response to that work. Thus no expression of faith in Christ is necessary at all. The forms of inclusivism I will here advocate maintain that some will be allowed an opportunity at some point after death to accept or trust in Jesus' atonement. One cannot be fully accepted by God without faith in Jesus. (Inclusivism is opposed to *Christian exclusivism* which would say that one must in this life express faith in Christ to be saved.) (See figures 3–5 and 1.)

Limited potential restorationism says that not all of the lost after death are unredeemable. After a limited period of punishment, some of the lost will again be offered redemption through Christ's atoning sacrifice. (See d2 in figure 3.)

I will also argue for one other form of inclusivism. Those who seek God and will to do God's will (John 7:17), or those who fear or reverence God and seek to do what is right (Acts 10:34), or those who do both, shall not be lost even though they have not professed faith in Christ during their earthly lives. One cannot be fully accepted by God without trust in Jesus' atoning sacrifice, but some who have never heard of him have no chance to do so in this life. Others who have heard of Jesus likewise will not have a fair opportunity to consider Christianity in this life. They will be offered the possibility of salvation after death but before any time of punishment.

I said that the Christian has the unavoidable task of demonstrating that the Christian God is not the devil. Indeed, we must demonstrate that the God of the Bible is absolutely good, loving, and just. If such a demonstration is possible, we will need to look at the relevant scriptural passages that bear on this topic and then think through the implications of those passages. We must also consider what we should conclude from that which is not stated. We will also discuss some of the philosophical problems and advantages accompanying the different views. Before beginning our biblical analysis of the afterlife of the lost, in order to have a sufficient background, we will need to understand the biblical view of the afterlife generally. But before looking at that, we need to think about exactly what it is Christians are about to defend, what the Christian should consider to be foundational to determine doctrine.

1

THEOLOGICAL FOUNDATION

Before we look at the problem of the Christian doctrine of hell, we should try to understand exactly what Christians have the right to believe and what they should feel obligated to believe. They should first be concerned to attempt to discern the most likely teaching of Scripture. Reasonable assessment of Scripture should alone determine doctrine. Sadly, even many Protestant theologians place a high priority on theological principles, confessions, councils, or Creeds whose statements do not always follow strictly from Scripture or reason. William Lane Craig, for example, in speaking about *perfect being theology,* believes that this is one important guide for doing systematic theology: "When the Bible says that God is Almighty, for example, this is to be construed in the greatest way possible, that he would have maximal power. Or when it says that God knows everything, we should construe this in the maximal sense possible and this will serve to then guide our theology in formulating our concept of God."[1]

Rather, Christian doctrine should be determined by discovering by sound scientific or investigative methods, and by seeking

1. Craig interview, "Ontological Argument," Reasonable Faith Podcast.

the leading of the Holy Spirit, the most likely meaning of Scripture to the original hearers. It should not be determined by applying any principle to Scripture not derived from Scripture or not required by reason. Perfect being theology may be tentatively professed concerning, say, God's knowledge or power, but it should not be posited as a clear certainty. Good exegesis may even lead one to affirm similar principles in some cases but not in others. Of course, reason alone will sometimes compel belief in doctrines not stated in Scripture. For example, I believe that prior to the creation, God was timeless. I think the philosophical arguments require this conclusion though Scripture does not tell us.

When the Bible allows for more than one of two or more mutually exclusive doctrines (say, A and B), either may be accepted even if current orthodoxy allows for only A. Here rational analysis must adjudicate, though the conclusion one reaches will often be inconclusive. For example, orthodoxy allows for only *ex nihilo* creation, creation from nothing. Creation *ex materia*, from material eternally coexistent with God, is clearly precluded by passages such as we find in John 1. But *ex deo* creation, creation from God's own being, is not excluded so long as the creation is not seen as divine, so long as God is seen as creating something which becomes other than God. None of the great creation passages like John 1 and Genesis 1 tell us which is correct. (Certainly the traditional proof texts for creation ex nihilo like Hebrews 11:3 or Romans 4:17 do not support this doctrine and they say little to resolve the problem.) Reason will sometimes lead one to accept one doctrinal view as more likely than the other if one fits the clearer understanding of the whole of Scripture than the other or if one can avoid rational problems implicit in the other. But one has no right to appeal to orthodoxy or tradition to resolve such issues.

Though we should certainly listen to and rationally evaluate the great theologians of the past, we should not accept what they say without question. Generally we should fully accept the great Creeds only insofar as they summarize the clear teaching of Scripture. Otherwise they are nothing more than the words of mere humans. They are merely human tradition.

Jesus commanded the early Jewish church to accept Jewish traditions that involve nothing more than harmless customs and which do not involve actual teaching or truth claims (Matt 23:2–3). But before giving this command, he made it clear that these human traditions had no authority in God's sight (Mark 7:8). At the time he did not appear to consider such traditions even worth keeping (v. 5) and, had the Jewish leaders not made this so great an issue of contention, he might not have later told his followers to do otherwise. He was very clear that human tradition that does involve spiritual teaching has no authority over Scripture, it should be rejected when it contradicts Scripture, and, indeed, it has no authority to be accepted at all (vv. 8–13). (In this passage the spiritual teaching found in the tradition stated that God allows certain earlier divine commands to be disregarded.)

Jesus taught that the Holy Spirit, the *Paraclete*, would later give his direct followers more information and that the Spirit would remind them of Jesus' teachings (John 14:26; 16:13). Thus we have reason to accept the basic content of the NT. Jesus' teachings are verified as inspired by the evidence of his resurrection and his fulfillment of messianic prophecy. Jesus also accepted the inspiration of the Hebrew Scripture. Much of the NT is made up of writings of the apostle Paul. Paul's words are verified as inspired by God in that the other apostles, those whose authority we have just established, confirmed his apostolic authority (Gal 2:2, 7–9). The Epistle of James may be in the same category. We have no good reason to think that any such authority to establish new teachings has been passed on to anyone other than the first apostles. Beyond the Bible, all else must be considered mere human tradition unless independent evidence for extrabiblical revelation can be given.

The 2003 film *Luther* has recorded fairly accurately the sentiments, possibly even some of the exact statements, expressed at the Diet of Worms.[2] Here Martin Luther gave the essence of his argument against the authority of human tradition.

---

2. Till, *Luther,* "A Simple Reply."

ALEANDRO: You, Martin Luther, will not draw into doubt those things which the Catholic Church has judged already. . . . You wait in vain for a disputation over things that you are obligated to believe.

LUTHER: Unless I am convinced by Scriptures and by plain reason and not by popes and councils who have so often contradicted themselves, my conscience is captive to the Word of God.

I fear that even many Protestants have in principle gone over to the side of Catholic traditionalism giving credence to councils, confessions, Creeds, and theological principles which they have no right to consider authoritative.

2

THE HEBREW VIEW OF
THE AFTERLIFE

THE SLEEP OF DEATH: CONSCIOUS, SEMI-CONSCIOUS, OR UNCONSCIOUS

To consider the doctrine of the lost and the saved after death we should look at a number of the important biblical passages which speak to this issue.[1]

Earlier passages in the Hebrew Scripture suggest that all people will experience annihilation at death, though most of these statements might be considered mere unauthoritative, uninspired popular beliefs common to the Jews (see Ps 30:9; 88:3–7, 10–12; Isa 38:18–19; 2 Sam 14:14; Eccl 9:5–6, 10; Job 3:13–14, 17–19).[2] Many of these passages might also be taken as suggesting a gloomy afterworld similar to that of the Greeks. Nevertheless, it appears likely that some truly believed in annihilation since it is often

---

1. I will begin some paragraphs with a biblical citation and then quote or summarize it. My hope is that this will allow the reader to more easily refer back to and find the passage to examine it when it is discussed in later portions of this study.

2. See Wright's discussion in *Resurrection*, 87–94.

rhetorically questioned, "Do their spirits rise up and praise you?" (Ps 88:10b). Even in a dark, depressing underworld, if one is even semi-conscious, one can praise God. Thus it seems more likely that many of these writers or speakers actually believed in annihilation at death. Here we should be aware that just as the Scripture records the lies of liars, likewise it records other beliefs of men and women which should not be considered inspired or necessarily true.

Genesis 3:19. God here makes an important though somewhat cryptic statement to the fallen Adam and Eve, "Dust you are and to dust you will return." On the surface this indicates extinction of consciousness. This may be the basis for the common Jewish belief that death does end with annihilation. But is this obvious? Might it be that God is here merely disclosing only what will happen to the physical body and selectively omitting mention of the future state of one's conscious existence?

Whether this passage is announcing God's judgment of annihilation or leaving open what is to come, the context appears to offer a promise of redemption. God was not pleased with the grain offerings of Cain but he accepted Abel's animal sacrifices which required the shedding of blood. Wouldn't the Jewish reader or hearer have understood this as saying that only the shedding of blood is acceptable to God to bring reconciliation and communion with God? And if one might attain communion with God, might this also offer hope from the curse of death and annihilation?

Adam and Eve covered themselves with fig leaves to hide their nakedness after they sinned. God instead provided a covering of animal skins. Might this not suggest that their sins, which brought about death, were covered, atoned for by God? Their own efforts were not acceptable to God to remove their nakedness. Only coverings that required the death of another could remove this shame. They had just committed the first sin and the resultant awareness of their nakedness would be the most obvious representation of sin and the shame of sin. The symbolism is just too obvious. The children of Israel would have understood this as meaning that only the substitutionary death of an animal sacrifice can cover one's sins. Leviticus 16 and 17:11 (n.b. 16:20) and other passages make it very clear that the Israelites did believe in substitutionary atonement.

Some likely assumed death to be annihilation for all people whether they were under God's atonement or not; some may have believed that God's atonement through animal sacrifice removed the annihilation of death; others most likely did not accept annihilation at all. The difference of opinion matters little. What matters is that there is a good possibility that the atonement God offered did remove the curse of death as annihilation. We cannot assume that just because Genesis 3:19 appears to be a categorical pronouncement that the curse of death is universal for all (as annihilation or any other form of separation from God for that matter) that it can never be altered or removed.

1 Samuel 28:3–25. Some very likely believed in a conscious or semi-conscious afterlife for the dead. For example, Saul inquired of a medium to hear from the deceased Samuel. Notice that Samuel does speak of his rest being disturbed, so from this passage it is possible that he was either in a state of semi-conscious sleep or possibly even a more fully conscious but dreamlike state. He might be speaking of complete extinction of consciousness though this is less likely. If one is aware of one's sleep, how can it be completely unconscious? Since this passage reveals Samuel's prophetic word from God to Saul and something of Samuel's disclosure of his condition after death, as indefinite as it may be, we should take this as something of an Old Testament (OT) revelation of the state of the dead.

Jeremiah 51:39b. "They [will] shout with laughter—then sleep forever and not awake."

Verse 57 virtually repeats this statement which appears to speak of annihilation for the wicked. But here the prophet clearly says that this is a statement from the Lord. So these passages cannot be as easily ignored as some of the others mentioned earlier. They fit later annihilationist teachings that have grounding in the NT. Christian annihilationists today believe in an extinction of the unrighteous following a time of punishment. An extinction of consciousness for the lost, or possibly semi-consciousness, could be followed by punishment which in turn could be followed finally by complete extinction. The forthcoming time of punishment is simply not mentioned. These passages are also not inconsistent with a resurrection and a final state of conscious or semi-conscious dreamlike sleep.

Isaiah 26:14. "They are now dead, they live no more; their spirits do not rise. You punished them and brought them to ruin."

The prophet is speaking of the wicked (v. 19). Much the same can be said about this passage as was said of Jeremiah 51. Also, it is very possible that this passage is speaking of some never again being allowed to live in this world (cf. Isaiah 14:9–21). So it does not necessarily deny a physical resurrection. The dead will not live, but their final end could be conscious or semi-conscious sleep as easily as extinction.

Genesis 25:8. "Then Abraham breathed his last and died. . . ; and he was gathered to his people."

1 Kings 2:10. "Then David rested with his ancestors and was buried in the City of David."

Abraham was the first to be said to be gathered to his people when he died. This was a common description of death for the patriarchs and others until Moses but rarely afterwards. David was the first to be said to sleep or lie down with his fathers. Other kings following David were also described in this way. Since David's ancestors were not buried in Jerusalem, it cannot mean that he was merely buried with them but that he was reunited with them in the world of the dead. Both passages could be saying the same thing whether they speak of a conscious dreamlike sleep, a semi-conscious state, or even extinction. Yet extinction seems less likely here. To be gathered to one's ancestors may be metaphorical language and to rest with them definitely is. But even if both are metaphor, they would seem completely meaningless if annihilation were the meaning. Why speak of them this way if there is no one truly there?

RESURRECTION

We see the idea of a physical resurrection of the dead in the OT as perhaps a closing climax of prophetic revelation.

Isaiah 26:19. "But your dead will live, Lord; their bodies will rise—let those who dwell in the dust wake up and shout for joy—your dew is like the dew of the morning; the earth will give birth to her dead."

Though this passage could be speaking of restoration of the Jewish nation, the more literal and likely understanding is physical resurrection of individuals. Indeed, both notions might be present.[3]

Daniel 12:2. "Multitudes who sleep in the dust of the earth will awake: some to everlasting life, others to shame and everlasting contempt."

This is the only other passage in the Hebrew Scripture which seems to fairly clearly speak of a physical resurrection. But it speaks of a resurrection of the unrighteous, not just the righteous. However, I will shortly argue that with the coming of Jesus, the lost, the dead who have rejected God, entered a state of punishment while those dead who were accepted by God awakened and directly entered God's presence. This passage could instead be speaking of these changes.

Some other OT passages may suggest a resurrection but they are far less certain. The idea of a universal resurrection at the end of the age developed during the period between the close of the Hebrew Scripture and the time of Jesus and it became the dominant view by Jesus' time. Jesus did argue for the resurrection but the biblical notion was more fully explicated by Paul. Christians came to accept Jesus' resurrection as the firstfruits of the final end time resurrection. The righteous will be resurrected at Jesus' return. The lost will be resurrected also though it is not clear that this will occur at Jesus' return.

For future reference, I will here include Paul's general teaching concerning the resurrection of the righteous. I would normally

---

3. See Wright, *Resurrection*, 116–17.

not provide these passages and this discussion until chapter 3 but I include them here so that we may see the more complete biblical view and so that this topic will not be unnecessarily fragmented or divided.

1 Corinthians 15:21–23. "For since death came through a man, the resurrection of the dead comes also through a man. For as in Adam all die, so in Christ all will be made alive. But each in turn: Christ, the firstfruits; then, when he comes, those who belong to him."

1 Corinthians 15:36b–37a, 38a, 42a, 44a, 51b–52. "What you sow does not come to life unless it dies. When you sow, you do not plant the body that will be, but just a seed. . . . But God gives it a body as he has determined. . . . So will it be with the resurrection of the dead. . . . It is sown a natural body, it is raised a spiritual body. . . . We will not all sleep, but we will all be changed—in a flash, in the twinkling of an eye, at the last trumpet. For the trumpet will sound, the dead will be raised imperishable, and we will be changed."

Paul is not here distinguishing between a physical body and a kind of ghostly spiritual existence, but rather between a soul-animated physical body and a spirit-animated physical body, a natural human life in a physical body and a body made alive and imperishable by God's Spirit.[4] The resurrection isn't merely a matter of going to heaven as a spirit when we die. It requires an imperishable physical body.

1 Thessalonians 4:16–17. "For the Lord himself will come down from heaven, with a loud command, with the voice of the archangel and with the trumpet call of God, and the dead in Christ will rise first. After that, we who are still alive and are left will be caught up together with them in the clouds to meet the Lord in the air. And so we will be with the Lord forever."

---

4. Wright has demonstrated this fairly conclusively in *Resurrection*, 347–56.

SOME IN PARADISE PRIOR TO JESUS' DEATH

The following passages from the Hebrew Scripture give some indication that some did not merely sleep at death. Indeed, they may not have died at all.

2 Kings 2:11. Elijah was taken directly to heaven in a whirlwind and thus may have physically entered directly into God's presence. Of course he would have to have been given some kind of transformed body since the OT strongly teaches that no one can see God and live.

Those who dislike the idea of God having a physical presence in paradise might consider that though God does not have a physical nature, God can still create a spatial presence in which God is physically identifiable. This makes better sense of the various biblical visions of God enthroned in heaven (e.g., Dan 7:9; Isa 6:1; Acts 7:56) than interpreting them as mere metaphor or symbol. Perhaps one might think of such a vision as simply a theophany on a higher level than any ancient theophany given to the patriarchs or prophets. That is, in heaven when we see God enthroned, what we may be seeing is rather God manifest in a physical location while God's actual or essential being exists outside of space.

Genesis 5:23–24. "Altogether, Enoch lived a total of 365 years. Enoch walked faithfully with God; then he was no more, because God took him away."

The story of Enoch suggests the same thing we find in 2 Kings 2. Unlike the other named patriarchs in this genealogical listing, we are not told Enoch's age at the time of his death or that he died. We are rather told that God took him, suggesting that he did not die and that he was taken physically to be with God.

It may be that to God Enoch and Elijah experienced something equivalent to death. If this is so, passages such as 1 Corinthians 15:22, that in Adam all die, need not be contradicted. But this is something we have no way of knowing with any certainty.

3

THE NEW TESTAMENT VIEW
OF THE AFTERLIFE
OF THE RIGHTEOUS

Revelation 21:4. " 'He will wipe every tear from their eyes. There will be no more death' or mourning or crying or pain, for the old order of things has passed away."

Whatever the final state and nature of the saints in paradise, it seems clear that they will have unmitigated joy.

PRIOR TO JESUS' DEATH, SOME ENTERED
PARADISE IMMEDIATELY AT DEATH

None of the above OT passages conflict with Daniel 12, Isaiah 26:19, or the NT teaching regarding life after death and the resurrection. If the metaphor of sleep is to be taken seriously, this is compatible with a more fully conscious but dreamlike state in which the righteous dead are aware of themselves and others and God. This also does not disallow the possibility that others are not asleep but are more directly and physically in God's presence.

Mark 9:2–4. Moses and Elijah, for example, were with Jesus and conversed with him when he was transfigured. It seems more likely that they were physically present with Jesus. Even if this were not so, they were likely consciously present with God and presumably had been in God's presence since their death or assumption into heaven.

Mark 12:26–27. Jesus said that God is the God of the living and not the dead and that he is the God of Abraham, Isaac, and Jacob. It is likely that some pre-Christian saints have been physically in God's presence since their deaths and fully aware of God and their own condition. This more obviously would be the case for Elijah in 2 Kings 2 and Enoch in Genesis 5 (above). It seems to be the case for Abraham (Luke 16:22, 25), unless Abraham only directly entered God's presence after Jesus' resurrection (as I will shortly suggest has otherwise occurred for all of the righteous). However, given 1 Samuel 28 and possibly Daniel 12 (above), it is likely that until Jesus' resurrection, the majority of the righteous dead possessed this awareness of paradise and God in a state more like that of a dreamer existing in a nether world.

SINCE JESUS' DEATH, THE RIGHTEOUS IMMEDIATELY ENTER PARADISE AFTER DEATH

Several passages indicate that since the time of Jesus and before the final resurrection, all those accepted by God will enter the presence of God at death.

Philippians 1:23–24. "I am torn between the two: I desire to depart and be with Christ, which is better by far; but it is more necessary for you that I remain in the body."

2 Corinthians 5:6, 8. "We are always confident and know that as long as we are at home in the body we are away from the Lord. . . . We . . . would prefer to be away from the body and at home with the Lord."

The most likely sense of these two passages is that the righteous will be consciously with the Lord at death prior to the coming resurrection of the righteous. However, they do not absolutely preclude the possibility that the intermediate state will be a state of completely unconscious existence or *soul sleep*. With soul sleep, one would not be aware of any passage of time from death until the resurrection. It will seem to the person in this state that one is resurrected at death even though much time may have passed from death to the resurrection. Now we know that time does not at all affect or limit God (Ps 90:4). Because waiting means nothing to God, millennia of unconscious existence could pass for Paul between his death and the resurrection and both God and Paul could still say that Paul is immediately in God's presence at death.

Luke 23:39–43. Jesus was crucified between two thieves. One asked Jesus to remember him when he would enter his kingdom and Jesus told him that he would that very day be with him in paradise. This passage clearly indicates that some will be with the Lord in paradise at death. We have no good reason to think that this does not generally apply to all of the redeemed.[1] Given now that Luke 23 shows us that at least one person will enter directly into God's presence at death, 2 Corinthians 5 and Philippians 1 (above) should be interpreted as providing the same teaching.

Luke 16:19–31. Jesus' story of the rich man and Lazarus tells us that the lost (or some of the lost) will enter a place or state of suffering at death. It is clear that this state occurs immediately or soon after death because the rich man asks Abraham to send Lazarus, who is now in paradise, back to his brothers to warn them to repent so that they will never have to enter this place. Because the brothers are still alive, we know that the dialogue is occurring shortly after the death of the rich man and Lazarus, and the universal resurrection has not taken place yet.

Notice that this is another passage that appears to indicate that the righteous immediately enter paradise in full consciousness of their condition. Also notice that Lazarus could have actually done something, taken water to the rich man, had there not

---

1. Certainly evidence for a purgatorial state of some kind for those accepted by God would condition this claim. Notice that the promise to the thief on the cross does not provide good evidence against purgatory, as some claim, since it may be that his suffering on the cross was equivalent to or worse than what he would have otherwise experienced in purgatory.

been a gulf between paradise and hades. So we must wonder how the dead may be said to be any longer in a state of sleep.

Abraham is apparently physically present with Lazarus. Abraham could have been here and in God's presence since his death. When Abraham died it was said that he "was gathered to his people" (Gen 25:8) and of later deaths it was recorded that they "rested with . . . [their] ancestors" (1 Kgs 2:10). If at his death or at some later time Abraham was physically present in paradise, he would have to have a kind of intermediate body. He then slept or rested only in the sense that his earthly body slept and it will "awaken" at the resurrection.

Probably the best understanding of the whole of OT and NT teaching concerning the dead who are accepted by God would be as follows: Before the death of the Jesus, most of them existed in a state of dreamlike sleep very much aware of God and experiencing the joys of paradise. (God has always been the God of the living.) However, because Lazarus (in Jesus' story) and the redeemed thief on the cross were taken immediately to paradise, it is more likely that after the death of Jesus all of those who are accepted by God are not in a condition of sleep but are directly present with God. It is likely that most of the righteous dead are given an intermediate body until the resurrection at or near the end of the age. Only their physical bodies may be said to be in sleep. Thus the resurrection passages, Isaiah 26:19 and (possibly) Daniel 12, are not contradicted.

Perhaps Elijah and Enoch and possibly some others are special exceptions to even this conclusion (see 2 Kings 2 and Genesis 5 above). Daniel 12 does not say that "all" will be resurrected at once but that "multitudes" who sleep in the earth will awaken. Those who have their earthly, physical bodies in paradise would obviously not have earthly bodies in a state of sleep. It may be that their earthly bodies were made into a kind of intermediate body which will be changed to a resurrection body at the time of the resurrection of the righteous. Or they may possess resurrection bodies now. Since they left no physical body on this earth, God could give them a resurrected body whenever God would choose, though presumably after Jesus was resurrected since he was the firstfruits of the general resurrection (1 Cor 15:20). Also, Matthew records some being raised from the dead at the time of Jesus' resurrection (Matt 27:52–53). So it is not impossible that some others now have resurrected bodies in paradise as well.

Of course it is possible that all of the righteous dead are in a state of sleep, even unconscious soul sleep, until the resurrection. My arguments to the contrary are not irrefutable, but I think they are more likely true than not. Nevertheless, if the saints sleep at death, they would more likely be in a dream-like sleep with full awareness of paradise, each other, and God. An unconscious sleep of the righteous is not impossible but the stronger evidence is against it. Also, it is difficult to avoid the conclusion that some are physically present in paradise. Otherwise, what would be the point of Elijah being taken bodily to heaven or Enoch never dying?

Some of these conclusions draw from Jesus' story of the rich man and Lazarus. We will shortly look more closely at this parable or story as it applies to the lost. But for the time being we should recognize that even if Jesus did not believe this story depicted the state of the lost or the righteous after death, his view of the condition of the righteous after death should not be different from what we have just concluded.

Before looking at the the NT view of the afterlife of the lost, we should look at one last problem—not, I think, an extremely difficult problem—involving the nature of resurrection bodies and the final abode of the righteous.

A PROBLEM WITH A PHYSICAL PARADISE AND RESURRECTION BODIES

Carl Sagan posed a problem for the Christian view of a physical paradise.[2] When Jesus ascended into heaven, where did he go? If, after he left the view of the disciples, he were traveling at the speed of light, he would now be only about 2000 lightyears away from us. Since he

2. Alluded to by Spong in Craig vs. Spong, "Resurrection Debate," pt. 2, 11:10–14:24.

had a physical body, he must have gone to a physical location. Possibly Sagan was not aware that Stephen claimed to have seen Jesus at the right hand of God not more than a few years after Jesus' death and resurrection (Acts 7:55). The story of Jesus' ascension seems to indicate that Jesus reached his destination almost immediately after leaving earth. That would make the location of paradise not more than a few lightyears from earth and probably less than a few light seconds away. If our telescopes get strong enough, will we ever be able to see this paradise within several lightyears or light seconds? Or was the physical nature of Jesus just an illusion or a deception? Was he a spirit who appeared as a physical body but then disappeared after he left the disciples' view and went to a heaven which is invisible to us? Christianity has consistently rejected this essentially docetic alternative since it denies the physical nature of Jesus' resurrection body and suggests deception on God's part (see Luke 24:39 and our earlier discussion of the resurrection). Even if Jesus' body was simply changed to a spirit after he left the sight of the disciples, this likewise suggests deception.

The best explanation might involve thinking of the problem along the lines of multiple dimensions. Edwin Abbott first suggested this idea late in the nineteenth century with his classic *Flatland*, the story of a two dimensional figure, a square, living on a two dimensional plane.[3] His flatland is populated by other geometric persons such as circles, triangles, and lines. They are only aware of each other as they perceive their one dimensional edge. They infer their two dimensional shape and position by moving around, toward, and away from each other and by observing changes in their size and brightness. They cannot observe or conceive of a three dimensional world, of up or down. Should a three dimensional being enter their world, it would be like one touching the surface of a paper. Should a sphere enter Flatland, a flatlander would perceive a spot appearing out of nowhere and growing in size as a circle and then diminishing in size as it passes through the plane.

Now suppose we have two flatlands, two 2D worlds, one on top of the other like two pages in a closed book. The inhabitants

3. Abbott, *Flatland*.

of each world cannot perceive the other. But if one inhabitant had the ability to move in the third dimension, it could travel to the other world. Likewise, if there is a fourth spacial dimension, there could be another 3D world like ours directly in contact with ours but imperceptible to us. To travel to a particular location in that world (W_2), one could first go to a given location in the first world (W_1), then simply travel in the direction of the fourth dimension, and then end up in the corresponding location in W_2. If the two worlds are directly in contact with each other then the distance one would travel in the fourth dimensional direction would be very short or even immediate upon going in that direction.

Thus when Jesus ascended into the clouds, he could have at any time traveled through the fourth dimension and entered a distinct location in the other world that corresponds to a location in our universe. Had he made this transition while he was still in sight of the disciples, it would have looked as though he had disappeared. Likewise, had Jesus merely disappeared when he was with the disciples, they would not have understood that he had moved to another physical location. Only an ascension into the sky would have led them to believe that he moved to another physical location which is in some way beyond this world. And of course, as I have said, this would be a possible way to actually move to that new location.

This is only one possible explanation. Let me suggest another. It is interesting that not long ago when the existence of dark matter was first postulated—the mysterious matter surrounding galaxies and galaxy clusters—speculation ran high as to its nature and characteristics. Some even suggested that whole universes could coexist in the same location since they are made up of such different matter. The person reading this book could be sitting unperceived at (or in!) someone's dining room table as they are eating dinner. Perhaps, while sitting at my desk, I am also positioned nose to nose with an eminent musical conductor (eminent in her world) as she leads an orchestra. So if this kind of model is true, one might enter another world (a spiritual world which is actually another kind of physical world) by changing into another kind of matter.

4

THE NEW TESTAMENT VIEW OF
THE AFTERLIFE OF THE LOST

PREJUDGMENT PUNISHMENT FOR THE LOST
BEGAN AFTER JESUS' DEATH

Some of Jesus' statements indicate a fully conscious state of suffering for some of the lost at death. We see this in Luke 16:19–31 above, the story of the rich man and Lazarus.

We have seen that it is possible that Jesus never intended to use this story to teach immediate postmortem punishment. It is often claimed that because the imagery and ideas behind this story were taken from Jewish tradition and pagan folklore and because it is a parable, we should not take it that Jesus actually believed this reflects what will occur after death.[1]

Though I find the arguments for this claim weak, it is possible. If it is true, this means that Jesus only intended to teach certain principles found in this story. He was likely saying that the people should not require extraordinary miracles to believe and that the evidence Moses and the prophets provided should

---

1. See Wright's claim to this effect in *Victory of God*, 255.

alone be enough to persuade people to live righteously and avoid sin. Also he taught that God values what the world despises and despises what the world honors.

But surely the story tells us more than this. Wasn't an important point that those in hades cannot enter paradise? And if that is so, then the context is likely true as well that at death some enter paradise while others experience a time of suffering.

If Jesus never intended to teach that suffering for the lost begins at death, then we should probably accept that those not accepted by God remain in something of a state of sleep until the day of judgment. They likely will not face punishment until after the judgment. We should consider this as a possibility. Second Peter 2:9 may indicate that the lost will be punished until the day of judgment but this is not certain in the text. Since I have given some reason to think that Jesus thought this story does reflect reality and that punishment does begin at death, let's assume this and see where it leads us. I will give more reasons later.

Because we have no good reason to believe that the OT taught conscious punishment of the unrighteous after death, probably the best way to reconcile both the OT teachings and Jesus' teachings is to posit such a change at the time of Jesus' death.

THE NATURE, DURATION, AND DEGREE OF THE PUNISHMENT OF THE LOST

Luke 16:19–31, cont. The story of the rich man and Lazarus indicates that the place of punishment of the lost (or some of the lost) is a painful place of thirst and burning one enters immediately or soon after death. We are *not* told that this is a place of literal burning or that it is symbolic of purely psychological suffering. We are *not* told that *all* of those who are not accepted by God are sent to this hades. We *are* told that those who enter here cannot enter paradise. We are *not* told that they will *never* be able to enter paradise. If some or all who are here can never enter paradise, we are not told that the suffering here will never be diminished or changed or that it will not end in annihilation. If the fire here shall never be quenched, we do not know that some or all the inhabitants will not be released to another portion of hades. Indeed, because this is a place of prejudgment punishment, many believe it is not the same as the lake of fire, the abode of the lost after judgment. It's fire is not necessarily unquenchable.

Mark 9:48 indicates that the unrighteous will be consigned to a place where "the worms that eat them do not die, and the fire is not quenched." The imagery is from Isaiah 66:24 which indicates destructions and thus strongly leads one to believe that the unrighteous are consumed and annihilated. The passage may simply be saying that because the worm and fire will never die, they will definitely fully consume the lost. Nevertheless, many before Jesus' time had come to associate the imagery with eternal torment. Indeed, Jesus' words are not incompatible with several options. The lost may be eternally tormented in a fiery hell (whether a literal or figurative place of burning producing physical or psychological pain), they may be consumed and thus annihilated after a time of punishment, or they may even be punished for a given amount of time and then released to enter another state. Simply because the fire is not quenched does not mean that one will forever experience such burning. The phrase "the worms . . . do not die" does *suggest* that this is not a literal, physical burning; otherwise, how can the worm not be destroyed?

Verses 49 and 50 then say that everyone will be salted with fire and that salt is good. Since this speaks of "all," it could indicate a kind of purgatorial state that all must go through whether Christian or non-Christian. Salt was used in the Hebrew sacrifices and is a preservative. Fire causes pain and destruction. Was Jesus suggesting that this painful, destructive fire was what would ultimately preserve the lives of people? Certainly many universalists would take this view. Many who believe in purgatory would also say the same thing with the qualification that this applies only to Christians or those accepted by God.

Was this what Paul was talking about in 1 Corinthians 3:10–15 when he said that our works will be tested by fire? Possibly, though it is not at all clear that Paul was indicating that any person, as distinct from their works, will experience burning or suffering. But if Paul did mean that some endure suffering when their works are tested and if there are some who experience inordinate suffering in this life, it could mean that they do not have to endure this purgatory after death. The salting fire for the Christian may involve trials they must endure in this life to become what God desires them to be.

Then again, the "all" may indicate only the lost who were cast into hell. If this is so, Jesus' statement that "salt is good" may suggest a purgatorial nature of their suffering. But it also does not preclude suffering as being penal or retributive in nature, that the lost endure the punishment justice requires. Indeed, to say that salt is good and that some will be salted with fire may simply mean that it is good that justice be done. Other passages we will discuss clearly indicate that the punishment of the lost is penal, whether it is also purgative or not.

John 3:16. God loved the world so much that he gave his only Son so that those who believe in him would not "perish." The most obvious literal meaning of this term is annihilation. The biblical terms translated *perdition* or *destruction* or even *death* (as in Romans 6:23) are so commonly used to depict the punishment of the lost that it seems strange that Christian annihilationism has historically been as marginalized as it has been. Eternalists will see the passages that speak of eternal destruction as metaphorical for the endless pain of the lost, the unredeemed. Universalists will often see them as descriptions of the irreversible destruction of the sin or sin nature of the lost which will in turn allow for their salvation (cf. 1 Cor 5:5).

Matthew 7:13–14. Jesus said that many go to destruction on the broad road but few take the narrow, difficult road that leads to life. Again we have the idea of destruction that fits more readily with annihilationism. We also have the tragic statement that the majority will be lost, even though we are not told here that this will or will not be a permanent condition.

Notice that this passage does not indicate necessarily that God foreknows our future free choices for or against God. With a hundred thousand years or more of human history behind him and with no reason to expect the following, relatively short, two thousand years or more ahead will be any different, it was very easy for Jesus to know what the majority of humans throughout history had chosen and would choose. Jesus had no need to exercise middle knowledge, foreknowledge of what we would choose if we are given the opportunity, or foreknowledge of our actual future free choices, even if such were possible.

2 Thessalonians 1:8–9. Paul here warns that God will punish those who reject God, "those who do not know God and do not obey the gospel of our Lord Jesus. They will be punished with everlasting destruction, shut out from the presence of the Lord and from the glory of his might." The concept of annihilation is present here again, but we also see a notion of separation from God. The biblical idea of the punishment of the lost often focuses on the suffering intrinsic to the condition of being separated from God. Being cast from the face of God may also have parallels in the biblical idea of being *destroyed from* or *rid from* "the face of the earth" (Gen 6:7; cf. Acts 22:22). So it may be simply speaking of normal annihilation. If it is eternal destruction, this means it is annihilation which is permanently irreversible.

But if the sense is simply separation from God, then one would think that something would have to be there for it to be separated from God. Destruction could not mean annihilation in this case. Perhaps the dual ideas of destruction and separation suggest a kind of alienation from God that is so devastating that it is very much like annihilation. The word here for destruction sometimes appears to indicate ruin or loss rather than outright annihilation (1 Tim 6:9). Notice also that if the translation "everlasting" is here appropriate, it is the destruction which is eternal. It does not say that the lost will be eternally cast from God's presence.

Here some might question whether the translation "everlasting" or "eternal" (literally "of the age[s]") is accurate. (The same question arises in Matthew 25 below.) It is commonly admitted that the noun *aion* can as easily mean *era* or *age* as it might mean *forever*, and thus the context must determine the meaning.

But eternalists and annihilationists often claim that the adjective *aionios* must always mean *eternal* and not merely *of the age(s)*.[2] However, in 2 Timothy 1:9 Paul says that God's grace was given us "before times eternal" (literally but given the eternalist understanding of the word aionios). But there cannot be a *before* an eternal past. Thus here as in Titus 1:2 it must mean *before times of ages [past]*. The same term in Philemon 15 is very possibly limited to a human lifetime.

The use of aion and aionios in the Septuagint, the second and third-century BC Greek translation of the Hebrew Scripture, also supports a non-eternalist understanding of the terms. The Hebrew *olam* was often translated as aion or aionios. Yet olam often meant merely a long period of time.[3] This was one of the primary meanings for aionios in common speech.[4] Clearly, the notion of unending time was not something those who used the term always had in mind. If it was, then unless it was brought out in the context, the speakers were definitely not concerned to indicate that it meant eternal.

I must comment on a very bad argument that I've known even very good apologists and biblical scholars to sometimes advocate. It is sometimes claimed that unless aionios means *eternal* when applied to the suffering or extinction of the lost after death, it cannot mean eternal when applied to the afterlife of the redeemed. Thus either the damned must be punished or extinguished eternally or we, the redeemed, have no assurance of eternal life. Thus it *must* mean *eternal*.

Any person who will dare to call oneself a Christian, once they see what they are saying, should be *ashamed* to give this argument! Paul said he would be willing to give up his very soul if it might mean the redemption of his unbelieving Jewish brothers and

2. John Walvoord, "The Literal View," in Crockett, *Four Views on Hell*, 23–27.

3. Preuss, *Theological Dictionary of the Old Testament*, 10:530–45.

4. Balz, *Exegetical Dictionary of the New Testament*, 1:47. See also Sasse, *Theological Dictionary of the New Testament*, 1:208–9. For a very exhaustive study see Ramelli and Konstan, *Terms for Eternity*.

sisters. How far has the church fallen into narcissism and egoism that so many today will willingly reverse Paul's statement without a tinge of guilt? We are willing to give up *their* eternal souls so long as *we* might have eternal life! Rather, shouldn't we freely admit that we have no assurance of eternal life rather than proclaim that the lost must (for our sake) have eternal damnation?

No, our eternal salvation does not hinge on this single word. There is at least one other phrase used in Scripture that assures the redeemed that they have eternal life (see Luke 20:36). But if there were none, we should be fully and *gladly* willing to admit that we do not know that we have eternal life!

For the sake of the argument, let us consider the possibility that the meaning of aionios is *everlasting*. Let us see where our arguments will lead assuming first that it always does mean *eternal* and then that it means *of a limited period of time.*

Matthew 25:31–46. In Jesus' parable of the sheep and the goats, he says that those who do not care and provide for the least of his brothers and sisters who are in need will be judged to go away to "eternal fire" (v. 41) and "eternal punishment" (v. 46). The meaning of the word *punishment* is significant. At one point in Scripture the same word is used for nothing more than the intrinsically self-inflicted pain that fear brings (1 John 4:18). Annihilationists will often see the eternal punishment as meaning a suffering that ends in eternal extinction since annihilation is also a punishment and fire brings about destruction. Note that the parable of the sheep and the goats, like 2 Thessalonians 1, also speaks of the lost as being cast out of God's presence (Matt 25:41; cf. 7:23).

Augustine claimed that in this passage aionios should mean eternal because in v. 46 "aionion punishment" and "aionion life" are juxtaposed. Since "aionion life" means eternal life, "aionion punishment" must mean eternal or unending punishment.[5] But this does not work if we do not first know that "aionion life" does mean eternal life. It may only mean life of the age to come and we must glean the eternality of this life from other passages.

5. Augustine, *City of God,* 21.23.

If aionios here does mean eternal, then we should notice that this passage tells us nothing about whether this punishment will change or be diminished to a weaker form. We are also not told that the lost will forever remain in the eternal fire but only that the fire is eternal. On the other hand, if this word does not mean unending, then we have even more hope that the lost will have an end to their suffering.

Revelation 20:7–10. Satan, the false prophet, and the beast are said to be cast into the lake of fire and to be tormented "day and night *for ever and ever*" (italics added). Here the latter phrase is *ages of the ages* which does more likely mean *forever* than the mere *of the age* (aionios) in Matthew 25. Being cast into a lake of fire must certainly be considered horrific suffering even if it is understood as metaphorical fire and merely psychological pain. It almost appears that this passage does not allow for any possibility of annihilation as so many other biblical descriptions of damnation do. However, two earlier passages tell us that the beast will be *destroyed* (17:8, 11). Because the normal meaning of this word indicates annihilation, to be tormented for "ages of ages" may mean a suffering that will eventually end in annihilation. On the other hand, the passage may be speaking of unending suffering with "destruction" being just a metaphor for the same. We cannot be sure which of these two is correct in the case of Satan, the false prophet, and the beast.

Now assuming the unending torment view, notice that we are only told that three individuals will endure this suffering. But since the beast and the false prophet might be symbolic of certain religious and political systems, we cannot be sure that we have any more than one individual who will undergo endless "torment" without annihilation. Some have claimed that even Satan is likely symbolic of an impersonal principle of evil or accusation or temptation. Though possible, it seems more likely, given the ways Satan is depicted in Scripture, that this is a person. The accuser who seeks to persuade God to test Job, or the tempter who seeks to have Jesus give in to sin is depicted as a person. This seems to be the more likely biblical view.[6]

6. See MacDonald, *Evangelical Universalist*, 106–32 for more detailed

More importantly, even if we have only one person who will undergo torment and even if this punishment will continue forever, as I mentioned concerning Matthew 25, we are not told that it will not change or diminish to a weaker form of punishment.

Revelation 20:11–15. Following on the description of the punishment of Satan, we see the judgment of the people of the earth. Those not found to have their names written in the book of life will also be cast into the lake of fire. Unlike Satan, we are told nothing about how long they will be there and we are not told whether they will ever be annihilated. However, annihilationists will point out that being thrown into a lake of fire does normally indicate destruction and extinction. We are told that they will be judged according to their works, according to the evil and good they had done. The punishment of some will be greater than that of others.

Revelation 14:9–11. Those who worship the beast and his image and who receive his mark will drink the wine of God's wrath and be tormented with fire and burning sulphur. "And the smoke of their torment will rise for ever and ever. There will be no rest day or night for those who worship the beast and its image, or for anyone who receives the mark of its name" (v. 11). We are not told how long these particular people will be punished in this way or if anyone else will endure this kind of torment. That "the smoke of their torture went up forever" (LEB) likely indicates that the memory of their loss will never be forgotten. It is a sign that their shame will always be on display, not that they will be tormented in this way for that long. This is the meaning we find for the same imagery as it was originally used in Isaiah 34:9–10 (cf. Dan 12:2).

Matthew 18:21–35. In the parable of the unforgiving servant, Jesus tells the story of a servant who was forgiven a large debt by his master but who then refused to forgive a small debt owed by a fellow servant. The master hears of this and then negates his forgiveness of the unforgiving servant. This servant is cast into prison

---

discussion of the problem passages of the book of Revelation. Though we obviously have significant disagreements, I must recommend his book for its very detailed and extensive arguments and references.

to be tormented until he pays all that is owed. Since the parable clearly deals with how we will be treated by God and forgiven by God, it indicates that the lost, the unforgiven, will leave a place or state of torment when all is paid. The master "handed him over to the jailers to be tortured, until he should pay back all he owed. This is how my heavenly Father will treat each of you unless you forgive your brother or sister from your heart" (vv. 34–35). This probably does not mean that the suffering ends in annihilation since release from the torment seems to be depicted as desirable and something of a return to a previous state which was lacking torment. But annihilation cannot be unquestionably precluded.

It is sometimes argued that the size of the debt the unforgiving servant owes is so great that Jesus' point is that the servant will never get out of prison. Craig Keener points out that ten thousand talents was probably more than the annual income of a large, prosperous kingdom in Jesus' time.[7]

But there is a foundational concept in the Hebrew Scripture that Jesus would have assumed here. It tells us that sin—at least most sin—can be paid for by suffering. This would suggest that no matter how great the debt, there is a way to pay it eventually. For example, God told Isaiah that Jerusalem's harsh punishment was ended once she had paid for her sin by her suffering. In fact, she had paid double for her sin (40:2)!

Getting back to the parable, we should also consider that if a servant was this greatly in debt, it may be that he had assets that were not enormously less than the amount owed (vv. 24–25). This is not the kind of debt that is categorically unpayable like the unpardonable sin, otherwise Jesus would not have said that the servant will not get out until all is paid.

Luke 12:42–48. In the parable of the watchful and unwatchful servants, Jesus told of some negligent or evil servants being punished with many stripes and some with few. Two servants may have done the same evil but one was aware of God's will and the other not. Some will be punished according to the evil they had done and according to their awareness of how much evil would

7. Keener, *Background Commentary*, 95–96.

result from their sins. We see a great variation in the degree of suffering of the lost.

The clearest sense of Jesus' parable is that there will be an end to the punishment. Few blows (or stripes) and many blows cannot be taken to mean an infinite number of blows. Clearly Jesus did not think the suffering would last forever.

Luke 10:10–14. Jesus warned certain contemporary cities which had rejected him that it will be more tolerable on the day of judgment for some notoriously evil cities of antiquity like Sodom than it will be for them. He said that these ancient cities would have repented in sackcloth and ashes had they witnessed the same miracles that the contemporary cities had seen. Since both will be condemned, again we see that there must be much variation in the punishment of the lost.

Jesus sometimes spoke of some being guilty of greater sins than other people (e.g., John 19:11), which indicates that some will be punished more than others. When he said that certain people, because of the magnitude of their sins, will be punished most severely (Luke 20:47), he implied that others will be punished less severely.

NEVER DIMINISHING SUFFERING?

Assuming Revelation 20:7–10 is not speaking of annihilation, only here do we have at least one person who will be tormented forever. If Matthew 25 is not speaking of annihilation and if aionios is accurately translated *eternal*, then it speaks of unending punishment for many people. Neither of these passages nor any of the others that tell us something about the horrific nature of the punishment tell us that their torment will never be diminished. Revelation 14:10–11 is the closest we get to such a claim. Yes, the particular group of people described here have no rest day or night from the harsh torment of v. 10, but we are not told how long this will last.

We have seen that the parable of the unforgiving servant (Matthew 18) does more likely indicate that suffering will end for the lost. But if we are also told that some punishment will continue forever (Revelation 20, Matthew 25), the best explanation would be that though some kind of punishment continues forever another kind will come to an end. Even if we did not have Matthew 18 indicating an end to some portion of the punishment of the lost, because we are not told that the punishment will never be diminished or changed, we have no good reason to reject this possibility.

The words translated as "torment" in the most important of these passages (e.g., Rev 14:11 and 20:10) is the same word or word form used elsewhere in the New Testament for nothing more than anxiety (2 Pet 2:8) or being buffeted by a storm (Matt 14:24). This is not to say that the torment of Revelation 14 and 20 is not harsh, but it does open the door for the possibility that it will eventually be reduced, and if it is, it may still be called torment. In fact, the mere lack of joy of the lost contrasted with the joy of the redeemed might be called torment. Thus the lost, if they eventually reach nothing worse than a pleasureless and painless state of existence, may still be accurately said to be in torment, and, indeed, endless torment if it lasts forever. Moreover, even if the lost are eventually allowed a specific kind of enjoyment or happiness, they may still be said to be in torment insofar as this state contrasts so sharply with that of the redeemed. As we have seen, much the same can be said concerning the word *punishment* in Matthew 25:46.

If we cannot accept that Matthew 25 speaks of *unending* punishment, then we would have more reason to believe that the punishment of all of the lost will end. Satan might be the one exception. But if his suffering is unending we do not know that it will not eventually be diminished or changed to a different form. We also do not know for certain that it will not end in annihilation.

Genesis 18:25. "Far be it from you to do such a thing—to kill the righteous with the wicked, treating the righteous and the wicked alike. Far be it from you! Will not the Judge of all the earth do right?"

Abraham contended with God, pleading with God not to destroy an evil city if as few as ten righteous people could be found there. The grounds for his appeal was simply that the Judge of all the earth will do what is just. Certainly Abraham was motivated in his appeal to save the lives of his nephew Lot and Lot's family who lived in Sodom. But behind this appeal is the foundational belief that God is absolutely just. We might question just how unjust it actually would be for God to take the lives of the righteous. Doesn't God do this every day? Since everyone has to die eventually, maybe Abraham was assuming that God always allows the righteous to live long lives. So perhaps he was thinking of the possibility of some *younger* righteous people living in Sodom?

Whatever his rationale, if we accept that Abraham had some grounds for his appeal, that his statement had some meaning, how much more might we think that God would never punish the wicked with unending, undiminishing pain. To kill a few righteous people would be nothing compared to this. Throughout the Scripture we see this basic assumption of God's goodness and justice. But we also see that it is completely incompatible with any notion of eternal, undiminished, horrific suffering.

Understanding the whole tenor of Scripture helps us to see that the punishment of the lost, even if it does last forever, cannot be the unspeakable horror that eternalism claims. The easiest way to solve this problem is to admit that their punishment will diminish with time; even though it may be eternal, it will be changed.

SOME NEVER SAVED

We need to look at some passages that appear to indicate that some, because of certain choices they make, will never be accepted by God.

Luke 12:10. "And everyone who speaks a word against the Son of Man will be forgiven, but anyone who blasphemes against the Holy Spirit will not be forgiven."

Matthew 12:32b. "Anyone who speaks against the Holy Spirit will not be forgiven, either in this age or in the age to come."

Matthew 12:31–32 is the parallel passage for Luke 12:10. The other parallel passage in Mark says they will never be forgiven and that it is an eternal sin (3:29). However, the terms used in Mark are *aion* and *aionios*, which, as we have discussed, may mean merely *age* and *of the age* and may not clearly deny an eventual time of forgiveness.

Because each of the Synoptic Gospels records a variation of this statement, we have good reason to believe that Jesus did actually say in essence that those who commit this sin can never be forgiven by God. But furthermore, it is very difficult to imagine that Jesus could warn his listeners about this sin and yet that no one would ever commit this sin.

Unrelenting rejection of God or refusal to accept God's offer of salvation could be the core essence of the unpardonable sin.[8] One may resist the Holy Spirit by *knowingly,* obdurately, and irrevocably denying that Jesus came from God to provide salvation or by knowingly refusing that salvation. By its very nature, one would never repent of this sin.

If it were some other sin or kind of sin of which one might repent, then whatever it is, since it is unpardonable, no repentance can remove it. We might recall that there are some sins which can be removed by enduring the punishment the sin entails (see our earlier discussion of Isaiah 40:2 and the parable of the unforgiving servant in Matthew 18). So unless this is the type of sin suggested in the previous paragraph, one might commit this sin, pay for it by enduring the suffering the sin deserves, repent of any other sins one has committed, and eventually be reconciled to God. We cannot conclude that we definitely know that committing the unpardonable sin does necessarily keep one from reconciliation with God and full acceptance by God.

I quoted Matthew's parallel passage because it is particularly interesting in that it suggests the possibility that some will not be forgiven for some sins in this life but they may be in the life to come. We will later discuss this under the topic limited potential restorationism.

---

8. See Instone-Brewer, *Jesus Scandals,* 173–77 for an interesting discussion of this sin.

Mark 14:21. "The Son of Man will go just as it is written about him. But woe to that man who betrays the Son of Man! It would be better for him if he had not been born."

Jesus said this to Judas. Judas did go on to betray Jesus, so we know that there is at least one person of whom it may be said that it would be better had he never been born. This can never be said of any person who is redeemed and accepted by God. If the lost should suffer punishment in the next life and then be annihilated or if they would continue existing thereafter in even a painless and pleasureless state, it could still be said of them that it would be better had they never been born. This is because the full sum of their suffering would far outweigh all enjoyment in their lives. But if after their time of suffering they in some way do come to experience the love of God, then it cannot be said of them that it would be better had they never been born. If, like the redeemed, they experience God's love for infinite time, that good will outweigh any finite degree of pain they had previously endured.

Given these considerations, semi-restorationism (as defined in the Introduction) cannot be true for at least one person, Judas. There is only one way that I can see that one might avoid this conclusion. It is possible that when Jesus said that it would be better had Judas never been born, he was speaking of only his coming time of suffering but not of any subsequent period. (See figure 3.)

With this issue, one is reminded of the way the Hebrew word olam is used in our Hebrew Scripture. Though it is often translated *forever*, it is so often used to depict a limited period of time that one wonders how it could ever seriously be thought to mean infinite time. Indeed, the basic meaning seems to be *uncertain in beginning or end or hidden*. The word more likely does mean unending time in certain specific grammatical contexts. But when such contexts are not present it is still taken to have some sense of endless time. Probably the sense is that, say, the "ancient (olam) hills" (e.g., Hab 3:6) haven't really been there forever, but as far as the reader is concerned and as far as God is concerned to reveal information about these hills, they may as well have been there forever. They have been here for so long that it seems like forever.

The readers and hearers had the creation account in the first part of Genesis so they knew that the hills were created at some point in time. It's as if God were saying, "It's forever, but you know it's not *really* forever. As far as you are concerned, as far as you can see into the past, it's forever."

Likewise, when Jesus told Judas that it will be better had he never been born, he was only interested in revealing information about the first phase of hell since that period was most crucial and concerning to him. It is as if Jesus were saying, "It will be better had you never been born, even if this won't really be true forever. As far as you are concerned right now, it will be better had you never been born." Considering the several passages we have looked at already, this wouldn't be the first time Jesus had mentioned a coming time of punishment for the lost without mentioning their eventual release.

If this is an accurate understanding of Jesus' words to Judas, we are left with the possibility of semi-restorationism for all of the lost. In Judas's case, we do not even know that it is impossible that he could eventually be fully reconciled to God.

Luke 16:26, cont. "Between us and you a great chasm has been set in place, so that those who want to go from here to you cannot, nor can anyone cross over from there to us."

We have discussed this passage earlier and I have claimed that this story does more likely reflect Jesus' beliefs concerning the state of the lost after death. It does not tell us that all the lost will enter this particular hell. I would be tempted to say that those who do come here can never be redeemed, except that we are not told that the gulf will *never* be bridged. Some universalists will claim that the gulf was bridged when Jesus preached to the spirits in prison after his death (1 Pet 3:19). I have argued that it is more likely that this state of conscious suffering did not even exist prior to Jesus' death and resurrection. Be that as it may, our main problem is that it is difficult to say whether Jesus meant that the gulf is permanently untraversable or that the possibility is open that someday it will be bridged.

Let me say just a little more about Jesus' belief that this story did or did not reflect the state of some or all of the lost and the righteous at death. It is sometimes objected that this is only a parable and we do not honestly know that there are any who are sent here. But it is questionable whether this should be called a parable at all. Nothing in this story is clearly metaphorical. Jesus was not talking about seed representing the gospel or servants representing his followers. Of course, we do not know whether Lazarus and the rich man were real people or imaginary creations. Jewish literature had a similar story from which Jesus drew. We may even question whether, in Jesus' view, the fire of hell is physically real. Nevertheless, Jesus' point was very clear that without repentance, anyone who committed certain sins would face very undesirable consequences. Of course, that much was already clear from Jesus' other teachings. But it is at least also likely that he was saying that punishment does begin at death for the lost.

It is difficult to imagine that whatever other sins this hypothetical rich man had committed that there are no other wealthy people who have ignored the poor at their gates and who are guilty to the same degree. Some exegetes will claim that the rich man was guilty of knowingly allowing Lazarus to die of starvation while he himself lived sumptuously. This would be such a very horrible evil that it might cause us to think that there may be many who are not accepted by God who will *not* be sent to this particular place or state. Still, as horrendous as this evil might be, it is also not difficult to think of people throughout history who have done even greater evils. This hell is not likely empty.

I have also noted elsewhere that it appears that Jesus is responding to several different views of the afterlife that were popular at the time. He seems to be saying, "Even though other teachers will tell you such and such about the next life, I'm telling you this. I agree with this view and disagree with that one" (cf. Matt 5:21, 27, 33, 38, 43). What Jesus is saying here about the next life cannot be ignored or negated even if it is only a parable.

With the story of the rich man and Lazarus, with Jesus' statement about the unpardonable sin, and with his statement to Judas that it would be better had he never been born, it is still not clear that there are any who can never be fully reconciled to God. Nevertheless, these passages, or some of them, may suggest to some readers that certain people will never be fully accepted by God—perhaps even strongly suggest it.

Revelation 20:10, cont. We have looked at this verse earlier and concluded that there is almost undeniably at least one person, Satan, who will be eternally tormented or annihilated. I also noted that if it is not annihilation, we are not told that there will be no change or decrease in this torment. But in any case, Satan will never be fully reconciled to God. With this conclusion, it appears to be even more plausible to think that there could be others who will never be fully accepted by God.

5

LIMITED POTENTIAL
RESTORATIONISM

SOME SAVED AFTER A TIME OF PUNISHMENT

Limited potential restorationism says that not all of the lost after death are unredeemable. It claims that after a limited period of suffering, according to the degree of punishment one deserves, some of the lost will again be offered redemption through Christ's atoning sacrifice (see d2 in figure 3). It's potential restorationism because it says that salvation may still be rejected. It's limited restorationism because it is not offered to all of the lost.

Though I cannot say this with certainty, it seems likely that some have in this life so strongly or repeatedly chosen against God and against God's will, and with sufficient understanding of God's existence, love, and goodness, that their choice will be eternally binding. On the other hand, there is some indication in Scripture that this is not so for all of the lost.

Matthew 12:32 says that those who blaspheme the Holy Spirit will not be forgiven in this life or in the next. This suggests the possibility that there may be others who will not be forgiven in this life, but they will be in the next. Some may thus endure suffering in the next life but later be offered forgiveness.

We have looked at Matthew 18, the parable of the unforgiving servant. We are told that this servant will not be forgiven and that he must be punished until he pays all that is owed. The sense is that release is available after imprisonment and punishment. (I will later appeal to this passage in support of a modified eternalism and semi-restorationism. See SR in figure 3.)

There is nothing inappropriate in thinking of God as again offering reconciliation to some after death. God offers us this reconciliation time and again before we die. Why should it be thought unusual that God might offer it again to some after death? Of course, this new offer of salvation cannot involve any fear of going back to any previous state of punishment if it is refused. The choice must not be coerced.

The above passages are admittedly far from conclusive. They are only suggestive, though I think strongly suggestive of the possibility of a postmortem and post-punishment offer of salvation. What is more important to see is that we have no good biblical reason to think that there can be no such postmortem opportunity. So we leave this as an open possibility. (We will shortly look at one biblical text which is sometimes presented as evidence that there will be no such postmortem opportunity.)

We should also recognize that the Bible is clear that one may only be fully accepted by God by accepting the atoning work of Jesus. Consider the following:

Acts 4:12. Peter: "Salvation is found in no one else, for there is no other name under heaven given to mankind by which we must be saved."

John 14:6b. Jesus: "No one comes to the Father except through me."

Galatians 2:15–16a, 21b. "We . . . know that a person is not justified by observing the law, but by faith in Jesus Christ. . . . If righteousness could be gained through the law, Christ died for nothing!" (TNIV)

Ephesians 2:8a. "For it is by grace you have been saved, through faith."

Peter's and Jesus' statements are very clear that ultimately no one can be accepted by God except through Jesus Christ. And Paul also makes it clear that it is by faith in Christ that salvation is attained. Notice that in Paul's statement to the Galatians he seems to be pressing the point that if there were any other possible way we could be accepted by God, God would not have required the horrible pain of incarnation and death on the cross. God would have taken any other possible way out. If we have any reason to believe that some may be saved after a time of punishment after death, then one must still profess faith in Christ.

Some sins can be paid for by bearing one's punishment for those sins, but ultimately no one can be fully accepted by God except through Jesus' atoning work and by accepting that work. Some sins, such as the sin of rejecting God or God's offer of salvation, cannot be covered by bearing the punishment those sins entail. All sin involves rejecting God since it involves rejecting God's will. Even those who do not believe in God, once they have an adequate conception of God, understand that it is not God's will to do anything that is evil. So the sin of rejecting God is still present after penal suffering. To reject God simply deserves receiving what is asked for, separation from God, even if the separation is eventually only a partial alienation. No additional suffering would be appropriate. Some may be given the opportunity to accept salvation after their time of punishment is over but they cannot pay for all of their sins by enduring punishment. Whether or not this rationale is correct, ultimately Christians believe that complete acceptance by God is possible only through Jesus because this is the NT teaching. This is what God has revealed to us.

To conclude this section I should point out that the Christian view of receiving salvation does not entirely consist of a simple act of faith, though that is the most basic step for entrance into God's kingdom. This has a bearing on our understanding of limited potential restorationism.

Our salvific choices (the choices by which we accept God's offer of salvation) in this life are made within the context of temptations: negative influences like oppression and even tribulation on the one hand and positive temptations of human desires on the other. The parable of the sower (Mark 4:3–8, 14–20) brings out this point very strongly. From the parallel passage in Luke 8, verse 13 makes it clear that many will be accepted by God but will then lose their salvation. It is also one of the main points of the parable of the ten virgins (Matt 25:1–13) that our ultimate or overall salvific decision will be made within the context of conflicting desires and pressures. In both parables many want to enter God's kingdom but ultimately refuse to do so given their final or overall decision in this life. The parable of the ten virgins also tells us that many will very much want to be part of the marriage supper of the bridegroom but will be rejected. They want a relationship with God but are unwilling to resist the temptations that draw them away from God. They are among the lost who are cast into outer darkness (Matt 8:12). Even though this will involve only a limited time of punishment, it will be a condition they will want very much to leave but, so long as it lasts, not be able to do so. If they truly seek and desire to know God, after this time of punishment many will be offered an opportunity to receive God's salvation.

Limited potential restorationism as described here may appear very much like the traditional Catholic doctrine of purgatory. I think that for many who endure it, it will be the same. But notice that it is different in that it says this purgatory will also apply to people who have never professed faith in Christ as well as many who have fully rejected God. Some will make a salvific decision after their time of punishment while others have already made it.

We should look at one passage that is often appealed to in order to argue that there can be no *second chance* for any of the lost after death. We will look at some others later.

Hebrews 9:27. "People are destined to die once, and after that to face judgment."

To reject this claim, some might respond by simply discounting the canonicity of the book of Hebrews. Hebrews was not written by Paul though it was likely from a Pauline circle, a group that had deeply absorbed Paul's teachings and may have had a relationship with Paul. Since this book does not have clear apostolic authority, perhaps it should be placed among the early Church Fathers. If so, it would certainly be the earliest and most interesting and informative of the Church Fathers.

But instead of pursuing this line of argument, let's assume the canonicity of this book. If only for the sake of the argument, what would be our conclusion if Hebrews is accepted as inspired Scripture? This passage primarily tells us that all people, at least all who have lived long enough to have done anything deserving of judgment, will not live on earth more than once. The passage cannot be taken as a categorical claim since there are clearly biblical examples of people who have died more than once (those raised from the dead by Elijah, Elisha, Jesus, Peter, and Paul) and examples of others who apparently have not even died once (Enoch and Elijah). So it tells us only that *generally* no one will live on earth more than once or after one death.

It also tells us that all will face judgment. Of course, the judgment for some may be that they will endure postmortem punishment and then have a second opportunity to accept God's offer of reconciliation through Christ. And we are also not told that there will be none who will be given another opportunity to accept God's offer of salvation after death but before any time of punishment or judgment. So Hebrews 9 does not really speak to the issue of whether any of the lost will have another opportunity to be reconciled to God after death.

GOD'S INFINITE LOVE

We need to see the biblical grounds for believing that God has infinite love for all people. This understanding will further support the argument that the time of punishment for the lost will be limited and that God offers postmortem reconciliation for some before and after that time of punishment. It will also affect our coming arguments concerning the final state of the lost.

If the time of suffering is limited and if God gives to each a variable degree or duration of pain according to the evil they have committed, then even if some have horrific suffering, it will be limited to exactly what justice requires. The primary channel by which God's love is manifest to humanity provides a means for us to never have to face the justice we deserve at all. But for those who refuse God's means of salvation, of deliverance from the justice they deserve, God can only give them justice.

John 3:16, cont. "God so loved the world that he gave his . . . only Son." We have looked at this passage earlier. This is the most commonly referenced scriptural passage supporting belief in God's infinite love. Here the sense is that God willingly endured something that was very undesirable to God, something that equated to enormously great suffering for God, in order to reconcile us to God. So much God loved us.

This is not a God of vengeance blindly pouring out wrath on an innocent son. The Son does not endure any more pain or suffering than does the Father. John 3:16 would make little sense unless this were so. Both God the Father and the Son had determined that this must be done to reconcile us to God. The decision was made by both. The will and choice of the Father and the Son are by nature the same.

Only when incarnate did the Son's choice at one point (in Gethsemane) appear to be not completely the same as the Father's. This was when he faced the temptation to avoid this suffering. But even then the ultimate choice of the Son was to do the Father's will. His prayer to have this cup pass from him was not disobedience, it was a request to the Father pending absolute knowledge of God's will. When God the Son became a man in the incarnation, his knowledge and power were limited and he was dependent upon the Holy Spirit to provide power or knowledge when it was needed (John 5:19; Phil 2:6–8). We might say that Jesus had forgotten that it was *he himself* who had decided that he must endure this pain.

This is not blind vengeance against minor misdeeds, it is justice that follows from the very nature of God. Any sin brings separation from God because God is completely holy, good, and perfect. God can have no part with sin. Because of God's nature, justice must be done and only a substitution which God alone can provide can avert that justice from falling upon those who have sinned. The suffering God endures may be very different from what a human endures but it is still suffering, and in this case unspeakably horrific suffering. And yet, because God so desired reconciliation and relationship with humanity, God willingly endured it.

This passage and similar ones like Romans 5:8 and Ephesians 2:4–5 are the basis for the belief that God has (theologically) infinite love for us. So important and fundamental was this idea to the disciples that in his first epistle, John would actually say that God *is* love (1 John 4:8, 16). Paul could express this idea with great emotion as well. He did this in the hope of evoking a sense of a degree and kind of love that was so great as to be beyond understanding:

Ephesians 3:17b–19a. "And I pray that you, being rooted and established in love, may have power . . . to grasp how wide and long and high and deep is the love of Christ, and to know this love that surpasses knowledge."

Let me bring up one other passage which very beautifully and emotionally expresses this doctrine. I will refer to it again later.

Isaiah 49:15–16a. "Can a mother forget the baby at her breast and have no compassion on the child she has borne? Though she may forget, I will not forget you! See, I have engraved you on the palms of my hands."

God's revelation to Peter was that God is no respecter of persons. God does not show favoritism for any person over *any* other (Acts 10:34–35; cf. Eph 6:9b). So Isaiah 49 does not say that God loves the Jewish people more than their neighbors or even their enemies who had oppressed them. The book of Jonah also emphasizes God's love for all people, even a people who were most known for their evil and oppression.

We also know that Isaiah 49 does not apply exclusively to the good or to the redeemed since the parable of the prodigal son and other New Testament teachings show us that God loves those who reject and hate God as much as those who do not (Luke 15:11–32).

The father ran to and embraced his son before even knowing he had repented. In Matthew 5:43–48 Jesus taught that if we love those who hate us, we become children of our Father; we become like the Father who shows love by doing good for the wicked as well as the good. Paul repeats this message of God's love for all people in his initial proclamation of the Christian message to the Gentile peoples who had never heard it before (Acts 14:17; 17:24–28). He carries over the same motif Jesus used of God's goodness and love being shown by giving them rain and abundant crops and blessings. He makes it clear that not merely believers, but *all* people are God's children.

This does not diminish the scriptural teaching that in some additional or special manner, Jesus' followers are uniquely children of God (1 John 3:1). Indeed, John exudes, "See what great love the Father has lavished on us, that we should be called children of God!"

Jesus exemplified his teaching of God's love for all people by eating with, relating to, and caring for those normally considered the most sinful people of his day. John 3:16 speaks of God loving the entire world, not just any special group and not just those who love or seek or obey God. God cannot forget us, any of us, and God can never cease to love us.

6

ARGUMENTS REGARDING UNIVERSALISM, ETERNALISM, AND ANNIHILATIONISM

ARGUMENTS FOR UNIVERSALISM

We have looked at some of the most important scriptural passages dealing with the state of the lost after death. We now need to look at other passages which are often referred to as evidence that all of the lost will be saved. With the passages we have considered already, and a few more we will look at shortly, very few serious biblical scholars will claim that the Bible teaches a simple universalism. Simple universalism says everyone goes to heaven, no questions asked and no punishment for the unrighteous and unrepentant. Most Christian universalists will appeal to a restorationist form of universalism: the lost endure suffering and then are offered salvation without coercion. Once they understand what God is like, once they see God's love and goodness and what is ultimately for their own greatest well being, all will inevitably accept salvation. For some restorationists the time of punishment or purgation is more a period of instruction though it is often admitted that even instruction may involve pain. Punishment is usually seen as pur-gative rather than penal or retributive.

We need to now look at some of the more important univer-salist passages. The following phrases in italics are added for emphasis. These passages are taken only from the NT. Some passages from the Hebrew Scripture that suggest or imply universalism or semi-restorationism will be mentioned later. Even if one cannot accept a full universalism, these passages clearly portray a final age of absolute perfection, completion, life, goodness, holiness, and joy.

Colossians 1:16, 19–20. "For in him all things were created: things in heaven and on earth, visible and invisible, whether thrones or powers or rulers or authorities; all things have been created through him and for him. . . . For God was pleased to have all his fullness dwell in him, and through him *to reconcile to himself all things*, whether things on earth or things in heaven, by making peace through his blood, shed on the cross."

Ephesians 1:9–10. "He made known to us the mystery of his will according to his good pleasure, which he purposed in Christ, to be put into effect when the times reach their fulfillment—*to bring unity to all things* in heaven and on earth under Christ."

Philippians 2:9–11. "Therefore God exalted him . . . that at the name of Jesus *every knee should bow*, in heaven and on earth and under the earth, and *every tongue acknowledge* that Jesus Christ is Lord, to the glory of God the Father."

Revelation 5:13. "Then I heard *every creature* in heaven and on earth and under the earth and on the sea, and all that is in them, saying: 'To him who sits on the throne and to the Lamb be praise and honor and glory and power, for ever and ever!' "

1 Corinthians 15:22. "For as in Adam all die, so in Christ *all will be made alive*."

1 Corinthians 15:28. "Then [when God's plan for the ages is complete] the Son himself will be made subject to him who put everything under him, *so that God may be all in all*."

Romans 5:18. "Just as one trespass resulted in condemnation for all people, so also one righteous act *resulted in justification and life for all* people."

1 Timothy 4:10. "That is why we labor and strive, because we have put our hope in the living God, who is the *Savior of all people,* and especially of those who believe."

1 Timothy 2:3–4. "This is good, and pleases God our Savior, who wants all people to be saved and to come to a knowledge of the truth."

1 Timothy 2:5b–6. "Christ Jesus . . . gave himself as a ransom for all people."

2 Peter 3:9b. "He is patient with you, not wanting anyone to perish, but everyone to come to repentance."

1 John 2:2. "He is the atoning sacrifice for our sins, and not only for ours but also for the sins of the whole world."

John 12:32. "And I, when I am lifted up from the earth, *will draw all people to myself.*"

Romans 11:25b–26a, 32. "Israel has experienced a hardening in part until the full number of the Gentiles has come in, and in this way *all Israel will be saved.* . . . For God has bound everyone over to disobedience so that he may have *mercy on them all.*"

Other passages could be cited though some only very weakly suggest universalism. The Ephesians passages might be speaking merely of Christ's sovereignty over all things, though this seems to strain its more obvious meaning. Romans 11:26 seems to indicate that absolutely all Jews will be saved, though this is by no means certain. But if it is true and Acts 10:34–35 says God shows no favoritism, then wouldn't this be said of all people as well? What else can having "mercy on . . . all" mean in this context? If "all Israel" does not mean all Jewish people who have ever lived and will live, then the universalist interpretation of v. 32 weakens. It could then mean having mercy by offering salvation to all. Still, if some of these passages confirm universalism, that would give more reason to think Romans 11 does as well. If Philippians 2:9–11 seems a bit weak to some because it says that every knee *should* bow, notice that Romans 14:11 says that every knee definitely *will* bow and that "every tongue will acknowledge God."

To sense the strong universalistic feeling that permeates the NT, it might be helpful to read through only the above italicized text segments. I have selected out these phrases and segments: "To reconcile to himself all things, . . . to bring unity to all things, . . . every knee should bow, . . . every tongue acknowledge, . . . every creature, . . . all will be made alive, . . . so that God may be all in all, . . . resulted in justification and life for all, . . . Savior of all people, . . . will draw all people to myself, . . . all Israel will be saved, . . . mercy on them all."

It is very difficult to argue that the above universalist passages in Ephesians, Philippians, Colossians, and Revelation do not *also* include the salvation of all demonic beings, including Satan himself.

We see that there are some statements here that are very difficult to avoid in their universalistic claims and implications. Thus we see a conflict between passages which seem to say that all will be saved and others that say that some will not. We will see later if there is any way this conflict may be resolved.

At this point we should look at some more philosophical arguments for universalism, though some of these do involve definite biblical evidence.

Often, Christian universalists argue from an almost Calvinistic frame of mind. Because the writers of 1 Timothy 2 and 2 Peter said that God desires all people to be saved, and because God's will cannot be thwarted, everyone will be saved. I find this kind of argument very weak. God can desire that no one would sin and yet also desire that everyone be free to choose. Rather than removing our ability to sin, God's desire that all be free is allowed because it is more important to God. Likewise God may want all to be saved and yet more strongly desire that all be free to choose. Just as humans may have such conflicting desires, one overriding another, so may God.

Universalism does resolve an interesting puzzle in Scripture. Jesus told us to forgive anyone who has offended us so that God may forgive us (Mark 11:25; Matt 18:32–35). It seems strange to be commanded to forgive someone God may never forgive. But if God eventually fully accepts everyone as universalism claims (either by forgiveness or by one's paying the penalty of one's own sins), there would be good reason for our needing to forgive. What right do we have to refuse to forgive anyone when God fully accepts everyone? How can we live forever with those we have never forgiven? Heaven would not be heaven. When we discuss semi-restorationism, we will see that it also resolves this problem.

Universalists will sometimes argue that if the lost do not accept God's offer of eternal life, God should eternally offer them the opportunity to choose to leave hell. Doesn't the goodness and love of God require this?[1] If the lost in hell actually choose to remain there, and if their choice is truly free, then so long as hell is experienced as even in the slightest way undesirable as compared to the perceived alternative, eventually everyone in hell will choose to leave. Even if there were no more motivation to choose for God than against, if one is allowed eternally, time after time, to make this choice, eventually everyone will choose God. At that point God will close the door on any further choices one might make and make that last choice binding.

I would want to claim that such a scenario is in fact a denial of the dignity of free choice. One is denied the ability to make an ultimate and final decision for oneself. If we make a decision that God does not want us to make, God simply does not accept it. We keep making choices until we make the right one.

Why should God forever offer an eternal cycle of choices to the lost such as some universalists request? Those who have knowingly rejected God in their earthly lifetimes or rejected God's will for them, if they have rejected time and time again, might God

---

1. See Eric Reitan's universalist response to a "progressive" eternalist position, the view that the lost are free to choose to leave hell but eternally choose not to do so, in "Human Freedom and the Impossibility of Eternal Damnation," in Parry and Partridge, *Universal Salvation*, 136–41.

not eventually say to them, "I give you as you choose," and close the door on any further decisions? Would it be wrong of God to do this?

I ask this as a rhetorical question, but not entirely. Under an eternalist view of hell, given the horrific nature of the state of the lost, it would indeed be wrong of God to do this, but not under semi-restorationism.[2] If eternalism were true, God would surely be little concerned about allowing us the dignity of a final free choice since by allowing it it could cost some people such horrible, unending suffering. This is one of the reasons eternalism cannot be true. God does want us to freely choose and God wants our choice to have significance. I would also tend to think that it would not be wrong for God to ask of us a final decision given annihilationism. But in this case it is far more difficult to say.

What we do know is that if semi-restorationism is true, God allows us the dignity of freely choosing our eternal destiny by rejecting or accepting God. At the same time God keeps us from the unending pain the spiritual suicide of rejecting God would entail. Universalism, even restorationist universalism, denies the ultimate dignity of persons; it denies that we are responsible to choose our own fate or that God will hold us responsible for our final choice. Semi-restorationism does certainly end with all people reconciled to God, but there is still a distinction between the lost and the redeemed and their final condition. The final choice of the lost is honored. The final choices of all people are honored.

Under limited potential restorationism and the inclusivism I will later advocate, there will be some people God will allow to freely choose salvation after death. But I find it hard to accept that there will not be some people of whom God will allow their choice on earth to be final. The judge of all the earth will do right. God knows who it is who has made their choices under inadequate information and who it is who has chosen with full clarity of mind and sufficient information.

---

2. See the Introduction for the definition of the term *semi-restorationism*. It will be defended and explained more completely in chapter 7.

They cannot have too much information either, otherwise again their choice will not be free. If it were clear and undeniable to all people that God exists and that one can never be fulfilled and know complete happiness without knowing and loving God, then many would not be able to freely choose against God. This is the reason most of us lack overwhelming evidence for theism or Christianity in this life. Too much knowledge can sometimes straightjacket free will.

But when we do have adequate information to freely choose and yet we refuse, though God may again give us many opportunities to choose, how can it be wrong for God to hold us responsible for our decision and to say, "No more, this is the last time I will ask you to come to me"?

It would be enough to have adequate information that theism or Christianity certainly could be true. We must ask ourselves, "What would I do if it were true?" Would we be willing to commit ourselves to and seek and obey this God if we knew it were true? Our reason for belief could even be so weak that we might even think the evidence for and against belief is equal—yet we might still ask ourselves the same question. And God's Spirit does move upon our hearts to ask this question. Only if counter evidence were so strong that we would not ask this question, then we would have inadequate information.

The final decision for some will determine whether they will or will not enter a postmortem, limited time of punishment, a time in which they must "pay all that is owed" and after which they will be offered again reconciliation with God (limited potential restorationism). For others during their time on earth, when God says, "This is the last time I will ask you to come to me," their decision will truly be final.

I will suggest later that there may be some who have a deep rebellion against God which is the result of forces outside of themselves for which God will not hold the individual responsible. But I also think that there are many who are fully responsible for their deep rejection of God. Their hatred is so complete in this life that God knows they will never again alter their decision. Because they have seared their consciences and are no longer free to choose otherwise, they will not be given another opportunity for full reconciliation.

I cannot say that I know with certainty that there are any in this condition. I hope there are none. Perhaps God will allow or cause them to forget their past memories and rebellion and, somehow, give them again the ability to freely choose. But then again, God may hold them accountable for their previous free and responsible choices. Whether we choose a million times or only once, if the choice is free, it is that one choice which makes us responsible and it is that choice that allows us to determine our destiny. Whether the final choice God allows us is before death or after, it will be binding.

We have seen that there are some scriptural passages which have strong universalistic implications. They conflict with other passages which tell us that at least one and likely more than one person will never be fully accepted by God. We will attempt to resolve this problem in the coming chapters. We have also seen that God must give us the dignity of free will, a dignity that allows us the ability to choose our destiny. But this same free will entails the possibility that some will ultimately reject God and never be fully accepted by God.

ARGUMENTS FOR ENDLESS DURATION OF SUFFERING FOR THE LOST

The eternalist will sometimes claim that since the lost have offended an infinite God, they have committed an infinite sin that deserves a punishment of infinite suffering. There are several problems with this claim. First of all, we have no biblical grounds for such a claim. That in itself does not disprove the claim but it does tell us that we will need other reasons to believe it or that we should consider it only very tentatively if we do so at all. Secondly, this idea seems impossible to fit with Jesus' teaching that the suffering of the lost will vary with the evil committed by each individual.

Thirdly, this claim confuses the modern mathematical meaning of infinity with the theological concept. God's infinity consists in God's completeness and maximal greatness in certain attributes, not in any idea of unending quantity. God is omnibenevolent because God is completely good and there is no evil in God. God is omnipotent because God can do anything that is logically possible to do. The idea of God's complete or maximally great attributes do not follow from any theological principle artificially applied to the scriptural statements. Rather, when they do apply, they follow as the most feasible inference from the Scripture itself. Whether a particular attribute of God does possess maximal greatness should be inferred from the relevant passages alone. But if God can be called infinite and if an infinite God has been offended, it does not follow that the offender deserves an infinite duration or intensity of suffering.

The most serious problem with the idea of a punishment involving infinite suffering is that this conflicts with the idea of a God of infinite love (in the theological sense). Is it even conceivable that an absolutely good and loving God would allow its creatures to be able to commit an infinite sin, a sin or number of sins deserving of infinitely great suffering? Any state that is undesirable, any state of suffering no matter how small the amount of pain, will equal infinite suffering if endured for infinite time. If God is infinite love (in the theological sense), God could not allow infinite suffering (in the mathematical sense). God's infinite love could allow a limited period of suffering but it could not allow anything worse than a subsequent unending painless/pleasureless existence, or its virtual equivalent, nonexistence.

Please keep in mind that when I speak of "unending punishment" or even "unending torment" in the biblical sense, I can mean (as per our earlier discussion) a painless state of being. When I speak of "suffering" I do not mean merely a neutral state but in fact an unwanted state, a condition which is to some degree undesirable. In order to attempt to speak consistently, in this study I will try to use the word "suffering" only in the sense of something definitely undesirable to the patient or recipient. Certainly a painless/pleasureless state could be a very undesirable existence to one who even partially grasps one's condition. But if God removes one's ability to be aware that it is undesirable, one will not so suffer.

Another argument sometimes presented favoring infinite duration of suffering for the lost is that neither Jesus nor his hearers would have assumed anything else unless he clearly said so, and he did not. William Crockett argues that the Pharisees, the largest and most popular Jewish sect at Jesus' time, taught unending conscious suffering of the lost, and their view would have been assumed.[3] But David Instone-Brewer notes that other views were popular at the time as well.[4] The Sadducees likely believed in no afterlife for anyone. Some believed that all Jews would be saved, with great honor given to some but dishonor to others. Some thought the righteous went to paradise, the wicked to hell, and those in between to paradise after spending some time in hell. The Jews of the Qumran community believed the unrighteous (including Jews) would be punished with suffering and eventually be annihilated. So it is simply mistaken to think that one eternalist view was accepted which defined Jesus' view.

Indeed, some of Jesus' claims (e.g., the story of the rich man and Lazarus) were likely responses to some of these views. We have seen that he said some will go the paradise, some to hell, and those in this hell cannot enter paradise. Of course, we have noted that none of this tells us if the suffering will not be followed by annihilation, whether some of the lost do not go to this hell, whether the chasm will ever be bridged, or whether the suffering of this hell will not be eventually diminished or changed. I have also claimed that some of his teachings do indicate an end of some suffering or a change in the kind or degree of suffering.

3. Crockett, "Response to Clark H. Pinnock," in Crockett, *Four Views on Hell*, 168–69.

4. Instone-Brewer, *Jesus Scandals*, 178–81.

AN ARGUMENT AGAINST ANNIHILATIONISM

Some have argued that if God created us, God has no right to allow us to cease to exist. Walter Sinnott-Armstrong, in a debate with William Lane Craig, gives a variation of the argument as follows:

> I take Craig's . . . claim to be that there is nothing mor-
> ally wrong with God killing anyone at any time for any
> reason, no matter how trivial the reason is. In this view,
> people have no more rights than mosquitoes with respect
> to God. Why not? . . . Maybe because God created us. But
> parents are prohibited from killing the children whom
> they create and nurture. Why? Because the children are
> separate people with rights. This reason applies to God as
> well. If God gave us free will, then He made us separate
> people, so why wouldn't we have rights not to be killed
> by Him needlessly? I see no good reason to exempt God
> from moral standards. . . . If Craig continues to insist
> that God is morally permitted to "take life as He pleases,"
> then his obstinacy will strike many people as desperate.[5]

Now it is not entirely clear what Sinnott-Armstrong is claiming. Does he think God has no right to *ever* take a human life, that
if God made us we should live on this earth forever? Does he really
think this? Craig's point is that however long or short our lives in
this world may be is entirely up to God to determine. God put us
in this world and has the right to take our lives according to God's
plan for us and the world.

No one has mentioned annihilation or punishment after
death as factors affecting the argument, so for the moment let's
assume merely that we will continue to exist after death. In this
case nothing is truly lost at death. If death is merely a change from
one state to another, it cannot be wrong of God to do this. Indeed,
even if God had no special plan for the world, God could take our
lives whenever God might wish for no reason whatsoever. And the
issue of suffering does not even apply though Sinnott-Armstrong
attempts to slip it in the backdoor, perhaps in the hope that we do
not notice its irrelevance to the argument. The issue of whether

5. Sterba, *God?*, 144–45.

God has a right to allow suffering is a very different issue from whether God has the right to bring about death.

So it seems that Craig's argument is very obviously correct. A parent has no right to take a child's life because both are equals. Even assuming that one's life does not truly end at death, one does not have the right to determine whether the other continue in this life or the afterlife. And one does not actually create the other. The couple's biological machinery produces the child with no true creative activity by the parents. The parents' only contribution to the process is the act of copulation. God, as the one who caused the world and all human life to be and who thus has the right to plan the course of the world, does have the right to take any life whenever God desires.

Whether or not Sinnott-Armstrong was thinking that death involves annihilation of consciousness, his argument could easily be extended to the issue of God causing one to eternally cease to exist. Some have used the illustration of our creating a conscious robot or computer. Does the fictitious creator of the fictitious android, Commander Data on the *Star Trek* film or television series, have the right to cause him to cease to exist? The very idea that one human can create another with consciousness assumes that by some special (as yet unknown) arrangement of complex parts, one can produce consciousness; that somehow a brain is just a very complicated computer that has passed a crucial point by which it attains awareness. In my thinking this is nothing more than belief in magic. No new arrangement of mindless material parts can produce sentience, awareness. An original, uncaused Mind must be the source of all human minds.

But let's assume that it is possible to make a sufficiently complex computerized android that it (magically) becomes conscious. Somehow by our arranging parts—wires, chips, photo sensitive cells—a conscious person is created. We would have simply rearranged material parts which had produced a person of no less value than ourselves and thus we would have no right to cause it to cease to exist than we would any other person. For a couple to plan to have a child is essentially the same thing. Built into our biological machinery is the capacity to produce new human organisms when a human egg is fertilized. In this case the couple does much less than even our fictitious android creator. One need not even seek to arrange computer parts. And this some would actually presume to call *creating a person*?

On the other hand, if we come from a creator as our source (Gen 2:7; Eccl 12:7; 1 Cor 8:6), if our conscious existence is given to us, then God should have the right to take back this consciousness or cause it to cease whenever God pleases. Our existence is not ours but our creator's.

Imagine being privy to the thoughts of God when God was contemplating the creation of humans (if, indeed, such thoughts occurred in time and could be translated into human words). God says, "I think I will create humans. I will make a biological machine that will metabolize and reproduce itself and mechanistically compute (reason) and I will give it consciousness." But now imagine that God says, "I think I'll let it exist for seventy years or so, maybe sometimes less, and then I will cause its consciousness to cease." Should we object? Should we tell God that once we are created, God is obligated to make sure that we exist forever? On what grounds? If our consciousness comes from God, is it not God's right to do with as God wishes? Can it not be taken back or extinguished if God so desires? It is obviously within our creator's rights to allow us to cease to exist if God so chooses. If Sinnot-Armstrong will not recognize this, as he says, "his obstinacy will strike many people as desperate."

7

SEMI-RESTORATIONISM

MODIFIED ETERNALISM: UNENDING PAINLESS/ PLEASURELESS STATE FOLLOWS PUNISHMENT

Looking at all of the passages considered thus far with the exception of the universalist passages and considering the theological principles that would most appropriately be derived from those passages, we may begin to determine the most likely state of the lost after death: First, one's deserved punishment must involve suffering of limited duration and intensity. But after that time of suffering is over, what then?

Well, assuming that aionios does mean *everlasting*, the unredeemably lost of humanity will have unending punishment. The annihilationist argument that the suffering of the unrighteous will end in the eternal punishment of extinction is admittedly very strong, though not discernibly stronger than the view that conscious punishment of the lost continues forever. Both views could be accepted by an honest student of Scripture.

If aionios does not necessarily mean everlasting in the passages which speak of the future of the lost, then we are still stuck with some who will be unredeemably lost. The revelation to John concerning Satan's unending punishment or eventual annihilation shows that there is at least one in this condition and thus possibly more. Under either a limited or unlimited understanding of aionios, the annihilationist and the eternalist views are both possible for either all or some of the lost. Even though we must keep in mind that annihilationism is a solid possibility, we will assume the eternalist claim that the lost who cannot be redeemed will endure unending punishment. I will here assume an eternalist view of unending punishment but argue for a non-eternalist interpretation of the nature of that punishment.

Continuing our summary of the most likely state of the lost given the Scriptures considered and assuming that the punishment will be everlasting, it would seem most likely that the limited period of suffering will be followed by a time of punishment that will involve no physical or psychological pain. I have argued that God's infinite love, goodness, and justice preclude anything worse than this and that no scriptural teaching indicates anything worse than this. We have seen that Jesus plausibly taught that the lost must endured only a limited amount suffering, and that no more will be given after that time. I have claimed that this second phase of hell can still be called a time of "punishment" and, indeed, "torment" considering how these terms have been used in the Bible and the enormous contrast of the state of the lost with that of the redeemed. I will call this our first scenario.

Let us consider a second scenario. If aionios does not mean everlasting in the relevant passages, then even though we must admit that some will be forever unredeemably lost, we have nothing that tells us that they will be punished or in torment for more than a limited period of time. So even if my weaker definitions of *torment* and *punishment* must be rejected and they must in all cases mean some type of painful or undesirable existence, we would have no reason to believe that any of the lost must eternally endure such suffering. Satan (and possibly the beast and false prophet) would be the only exceptions since "ages of the ages" could mean *forever* in Revelation 20:10 or (as we have seen) their suffering could end in annihilation.[1]

This is a very important alternate conclusion and we should not miss this point. So let me reiterate. If the words for *torment* and *punishment* must mean even very harsh, never diminishing pain and if aionios means a long but limited period of time in the passages being considered (as it most likely does), then all of the lost except for Satan cannot be said to be punished or suffer forever. And in this case we do not know that Satan's punishment will not end in annihilation. The lost, other than Satan, may then end in the painless/pleasureless state we have concluded for our first scenario.

Given either scenario, will the lost remain in a completely painless/pleasureless state? All joy must ultimately come from God. People who reject God may in this life still have some happiness as a kind of lingering residue of their nature as being created in the image of God. So long as we are in any way related to God, we may have some enjoyment or pleasure. But once the divorce is complete, one can have no happiness. Unless the lost can be caused in some possible way to relate to God, they will remain in a painless, pleasureless state for eternity. Those who reject their creator and source lack any deserved positive joy. If and only if God's infinite love either requires or allows God to choose that they be given a relationship with God, would they have this joy.

This condition of separation from God is admittedly little different from not existing at all and some may think that annihilation is a better alternative. It probably would be if that were the end of the story. But there is another issue we need to consider that may allow us to alter this modified eternalism even further. This factor involves the very nature of God's infinite love.

1. Hereafter, to avoid complicating my sentences, when I speak of the punishment of the devil and include the false prophet and the beast as possible additional recipients of this punishment, I will simply speak of *Satan* and use this term to include these three.

THE PROBLEM OF LOST LOVED ONES

The problem of lost loved ones provides reason to think that even annihilationism and modified eternalism are inadequate. Let me give a little background for this problem from its roots in the more general problem of evil.

In dealing with the general problem of pain as a difficulty for belief in God, I have elsewhere argued that the most fundamental biblical theodicy is what we might call a *recipient oriented free will theodicy*. A theodicy is an explanation of God's reason for allowing evil. This theodicy claims that God allows much undeserved evil to occur, both moral and natural, in order to test us as to our choice as we endure suffering. The evil is negated while the purpose for having the evil is fulfilled. (Moral evil is the evil conscious agents cause each other; natural evil is suffering caused by non-intelligent forces of nature.) Other biblical theodicies are sometimes needed to supplement this theodicy, however, depending on the evil being considered. This theodicy asks, "When we endure undeserved suffering, will we reject the God who yet deserves our commitment and love or will we hold to our commitment? Will we say with Job, 'Though he slay me, yet will I trust in him'?" (Job 13:15 KJV).

God desires to know what our choice for or against God will be and cannot without our making that choice. Also, as we make that choice, we become good or evil in such a way that we could not be without making the choice. A greater good occurs as we freely make that choice than if we make no choice. If we choose to cling to God, we will then have freely chosen the good. This is the greater good. If we reject God, then though this is evil, a good will also occur. It's a lesser good than had we not rejected God but a greater good than had we not freely chosen at all. The point is that even if we choose to do the evil of rejecting God, this is better than if we do not freely choose at all.

God could control our every choice but God wants us to have the dignity of free will, of being responsible for our actions. It is better that we freely choose God than that we be forced or determined to do so. It is most important to God to know how we will freely choose and it is most important to ourselves that we become good or evil by our free choice.

God allows us pain on the possibility that we will choose to cling to God, the God who yet deserves our commitment, in the face of this suffering. God allows this on just the possibility of obtaining such an enormously great good. This decision to choose God in the face of suffering or loss is the greatest moral good. This choice is the highest moral test which produces the highest good of its kind.

All undeserved suffering we receive will be compensated, sometimes to the point that it will far outweigh the suffering endured. So the evil of the suffering itself will be negated while its purpose is yet fulfilled.

Here we might look at the problem of pain as it involves the death of a child. The parent who loses a child will have the child back someday and the real testing, for the parent, involves being willing to wait and not to reject God for allowing this. But this is true only if both the parent and child accept God and God's plan for them and are thus accepted by God. Of course, the same problem confronts any two people who love each other whether they be a parent and child, husband and wife, or even close friends or relatives; and it often doesn't matter whether one has died prematurely or not.

A biblical Christianity would claim that there are some who reject God and God's plan for them and thus will be rejected by God. Our initial understanding of much of the scriptural teaching is that some of the lost will never be reunited with their loved ones and with God. Even if a couple, both of whom have rejected God, should reunite in hell, there will be no love between the two and no joy in the meeting.

A parent's suffering through the loss of a child fulfills part of God's plan and purpose for the parent. The suffering will be recompensed if each carry out their moral obligations and responsibility: if they remain committed to the God who yet deserves their commitment and if they do not allow the suffering to cause them to otherwise do evil. God offers a way for the suffering to be negated. If either should refuse it and reject God (say out of anger at God for allowing the suffering), they would have only themselves to blame for any continued suffering. For either or both individuals, an undeserved suffering can become a deserved suffering and what could have been compensated will not be.

This brings us to the problem of lost loved ones. If one is faithful to God and the other is not, then both will be separated. How, then, can God "wipe away every tear" of the redeemed (Rev 21:4)? There are few issues more difficult to confront than this. How can a person face the possibility that another may choose to separate oneself from one who loves that person intensely, completely, and unconditionally? It is the greatest anguish of all to know that any person is able, should they choose, to commit spiritual suicide. For our full reconciliation with God, we must freely choose to embrace God. If we reject God, God must honor our decision—God cannot force our will. This anguish, knowing that one may choose to be eternally separated from us, is an anguish that must be felt in the very depths of God's being.

This is one source of anguish that pushes many to continue to hope that some form of universalism or restorationism might be true. It looks as though some of us must come to accept the rejection, and thus the separation for eternity, of those we love more than our very lives. If we should ever come to love as God loves, how can there be any person who is lost for whom we and God shall not forever remain in intense anguish of soul?

How many parents have looked into the eyes of their newborn child and have felt compelled to love that child? How many have made an unspoken vow, "No matter what you become, no matter what you do, I will *always* love you"? Robert Munsch's children's book, *Love You Forever*, portrays very emotionally this absolute and unconditional love of a mother for her child. In the book the child grows and, like the mother who never ceases to love her son, he never ceases to love his mother. As a baby and then as a child, he sleeps in his mother's arms as she rocks him and sings to him, "I will love you forever." And when the mother grows too old and frail to sing to him, he takes his mother in his arms and sings to her, "I will love you forever."

Now imagine that we change the story. The child grows but comes to hate his mother. She endures a lifetime of rejection, ridicule, sometimes even abuse and violence. The mother still loves her child. She remembers the innocent baby she held and rocked in her arms. She does not love the evil he has chosen that now controls his life and shows itself whenever they meet. She is angry at the child when she sees him abuse, humiliate, and harm others. That anger might even be called hatred because his willful, merciless harm of others is so flagrant. But beneath the son's evil, anger, and hatred is the core of a person she cannot forget and she cannot help but love.

We have looked at Isaiah 49:15–16 earlier. It confirms that this is exactly how the God of the Bible loves all people. Even if a mother could forget and reject her newborn baby, God will never forget or cease to love any of God's creation. God says, "I have carved you upon the palms of my hands." The point of the passage is that God *cannot* forget us. This was originally written to a people who had rejected and scorned their God and on whom God had poured out judgment and destruction. When God's wrath is poured out we may even say that God hates the wicked (Rom 9:13); that God hates them because they have freely chosen this evil, this abuse and harm to others which they do not deserve. This may not be hatred as we normally think of it but rather merely a form of anger. But whether it is or not, it is not incompatible with God loving the wicked as well. Just as a parent may be angry at the premeditated evil choice of an older child and hate what the child has become and even in some way hate the child for freely and willfully choosing to bring this harm to others, so the parent will also love the child. God promised the Jewish people that though judgment must come, mercy will follow. Wrath, even God's hatred, ends after sin and punishment ends.

Lamentations 3:31–33. "For no one is cast off by the Lord forever. Though he brings grief, he will show compassion, so great is his unfailing love. For he does not willingly bring affliction or grief to anyone."

Psalm 30:5. "For his anger lasts only a moment, but his favor lasts a lifetime; weeping may stay for the night, but rejoicing comes in the morning."

Does this promise of mercy after judgment apply to the lost who can never be redeemed? Since we are told that God has mercy on all people (Rom 11:32), surely it must. Because God loves all people, as Jeremiah and the Psalmist say, somehow, for all who endure judgment, mercy must follow.

Our problem comes with attempting to understand how mercy might follow judgment if the Scriptures tell us that the unredeemably lost will be punished forever and estranged from God forever. Even if this punishment and estrangement consists of a painless/pleasureless state, how can joy come in the morning for those who are "punished forever"?

SEMI-RESTORATIONISM: PARTIAL RECONCILIATION WITH GOD

I can imagine only one possible way this problem can be adequately resolved: by the doctrine of semi-restorationism (SR, figure 3). As I have mentioned earlier, imagine first that the unredeemably lost had after a time of punishment reached a completely painless and pleasureless state (modified eternalism). Once one's sin is removed by punishment, the only sin that remains, the sin that cannot be removed by suffering, is rejection of God. It could have been removed by seeking forgiveness, but since it was not, it remains a stain on the soul of the lost. But God will not allow the lost to remain in a final painless, pleasureless state. As a kind of final if only partial redemption, God will alter their nature and allow the lost to experience the love of God and the redeemed. This would be far removed from the experience of the fullness of love the redeemed will know. God will have to take from them virtually all memory of their former existence. It may be that they will retain some memories of how they had loved and were loved

65

insofar as these memories would fit or facilitate their forthcoming experiences. They must also be aware of the special honor God bestows upon the righteous whom they will soon encounter, as well as the honor, glory, greatness, holiness, goodness, love, and worth of God.

God must also take from them the ability to freely choose so that they cannot refuse to receive or to give love. They cannot reject God or the saints. There must remain no memory that would draw them, had they retained their freedom, to rebel against God or against any others who love them. Such memories in someone who cannot again rebel against God would only bring discontent and anguish. There must be no memories that will cause pain, regret, or anxiety. They will be the same persons yet with the context of their previous powers and the memories of their previous lives removed. They will be almost semi-human or X-human. Only in this way will they be brought to know the joy of loving and being loved by God and the redeemed. All evil is purged from them and they are now unable to sin. They love and they receive love because this is what their God-created nature requires of them and they are now unable to choose against it.

Even though they may still be said to be forever in *torment* because of the contrast of their condition with that of the redeemed and because of their amnesia and incomplete relatedness to God and their incomplete being, still it is better that they exist in this state than that they not exist at all. The punishment Jesus said Judas would bear, that it would be better had he never been born, must apply only to the first phase of hell. It cannot be said of one who will forever love God and experience the love of God.

The lost may also be said to be *destroyed* in the sense that so many of their capacities and memories are removed. The kind of being they were before is destroyed. They are still persons, but in a less complete state of being. Also, their previous limited time of suffering and punishment could be spoken of as a kind of destruction and loss. So semi-restorationism would resolve the difficulty of reconciling those passages which may indicate some being tormented forever with those passages that speak of the annihilation of the lost.

Earlier I mentioned that if the term translated *eternal* actually means *of the age to come*, and thus a limited period of time, then we should expect that the time of *punishment* and *torment* will be limited for all of the lost. We have seen that Satan would be the only exception and he may eventually be annihilated. In this case, the lost, after their limited time of suffering and punishment, need not even be said to be in *torment* or *punishment*. Even if these terms imply great pain and suffering, they all come to an end.

The lost will not lose their eternal shame since this is what they had chosen for so long as God had allowed them their freedom. They will have no knowledge of this shame as they had during their previous postmortem time of suffering. Knowledge of one's shame brings a kind of suffering but after the first phase of hell, all suffering has been completed.

It might be interesting to look again at Daniel 12 in that this is one of the only passages which speak of the punishment of shame for the resurrected lost and it mentions no other punishment. It is commonly taken to be one of the only OT passages which clearly prophecy a resurrection of the the righteous and the lost, though we have seen that it might rather be speaking of changes that occurred among the dead at the time of Jesus' resurrection. In either case it could also be speaking of the final end of all people. Like Paul's almost enigmatic statements about God being all in all in the end, and all things being reconciled back to God, and God bringing unity to all things, might this, one of the last of the greatest prophecies of the Hebrew Scripture, be speaking about the final state of humanity?

Unlike so many passages that foretell only the intermediate period of suffering for the unrighteous, this passages might be telling us that in the end all that remains for them is not continued suffering but a state of dishonor. Here we are told of the ultimate punishment for the lost and reward for the righteous: ignominy for one and honor for the other. Other rewards remain for the righteous and another punishment remains for the lost (the punishment of their truncated being, though of that, too, they will be unaware). But other than the more crucial characteristic of being in loving relationship with God, shame and honor define the essence of the final state for all conscious created beings.

The plight of the redeemed who have lost loved ones is now resolved. All those who have come to learn to love all others as God loves them would face the same difficulty and find the same resolution. God's plight, because God loves more than any human ever could possibly love, would also be resolved. God cannot forget or cease to love those who have forsaken God. God cannot reject the children, the creation of God's hand. They cannot be fully redeemed or reconciled to God because when they had their freedom, they chose to reject God's love. But now they are given a minimal existence in which they are brought to know something of God's love and to love God. Their existence is good, but their final end will never be as fulfilled and complete as it could have been. And had they so chosen, they could have avoided so much suffering. They will be as fulfilled and complete as such a person can be.

I have earlier mentioned how universalism resolves a problem in Scripture. Semi-restorationism likewise solves this problem. "Why must we forgive those God will not forgive unless they will in fact eventually be forgiven or fully accepted by God?" the universalist will ask. Under semi-restorationism, because the redeemed will eternally relate to and love the unredeemably lost, they must forgive them, even though God will not forgive them. Only God need not forgive them and yet be able to relate to them and love them. Our unforgiveness for someone keeps us from being able to love them perfectly.

Semi-restorationism also answers a problem raised by the universalistic passages we have looked at. Under eternalism, how can all things be reconciled to God as some of these passages claim? How can all things be brought to unity under Christ? With the end of the age, God will bring about the perfection of the ages. God will in the end be all in all. Eternalism requires a hideous cancer to remain a part of the cosmos, a hell of unending pain and sin and hatred of God and others. Annihilationism solves this problem with a final end of all suffering and hatred. Likewise universalism ends with a perfect world in which all evil is gone and all know and relate to and love God. But semi-restorationism would also resolve this problem. In the end, the lost find the joy of God's love and all creation is essentially reconciled to God. Certainly the lost will forever bear their shame, it will be a mark on all who have rejected God. Nevertheless, because they will eternally know God's love, all will relate to God and God will be all in all. All of existence will in the end be good, sinless, and perfect. Though the lost will not be as complete as they could have been, they will be perfect in the reduced state God has recreated them to be.

Semi-restorationism does not completely apply to all of the universalistic passages listed previously but it does fit many of them. Other responses must be found for some of these passages. For example, Jesus' death can be a ransom for all people and an atoning sacrifice for the whole world without all people accepting it. It may be that in the final eternal phase of punishment, when the lost lose their ability to freely choose and are brought back into relationship with God, they will at last bow to Christ and confess him as Lord. And 1 Corinthians 15:22 may be telling us that in some way that we do not fully understand, even the lost who will never be fully reconciled to God will be made alive and know God's love because of the atonement.

Now there is one passage for which I find it difficult to avoid a universalist conclusion. In Romans 5:18, if one righteous act resulted in justification and life for all, does this not mean that no one will be lost? Exegetes disagree as to whether this passage does or does not speak of all people. However, I believe that the universalist arguments are more likely correct.[2] Assuming that the universalist interpretation is correct, the problem is that under

---

2. For an important universalist argument with responses see Thomas Talbott's essay in Parry and Partridge, *Universal Salvation?*, 18–22, 25–28, 251–59. I. Howard Marshall provides non-universalist arguments in chapter 4. See also Moo, *Wycliffe Commentary*, 353–57, n.b. 356–57, for non-universalist exegetical arguments.

semi-restorationism the unredeemably lost will not be justified before God and yet Romans 5 says they will. Do some Scriptures teach that some will be lost with no possibility of redemption and others that no one will be lost?

I tend to think that much of this problem can be resolved by recognizing that the difficulty resides in the language I would like to use. Under semi-restorationism the unredeemably lost will be reconciled to God in the sense that they will relate to God and experience God's love and love God. No sin remains in them except the prior sin of rejecting God, and they are no longer able to commit this sin or even remember their prior choice to do so. Since they are no longer able to reject God, it is questionable to what degree that sin may be said to reside in them. Perhaps God sees them as stained with this sin in that they had ultimately chosen this sin when they were free to choose. But God also sees them as a new creature in that they are no longer able to do this or any other evil. They would be seen by God as innocent and yet stained with the evil of their prior choices. In what sense then does sin still reside in such an innocent one?

They are alive to God but I would not want to say that they are justified before God. Justification, it seems to me, is a concept that should be reserved for those who have freely accepted God's offer of salvation, those who are fully and completely accepted by God and who have their sins removed. Was Paul not aware of the constraints I think should be applied to the term? More likely, I doubt very much that he would have cared how I or anyone else (other than God) might think he should use his terms. If, in any way, Paul did have in mind that the lost are *in some way* eternally alienated from God and yet relate to God in love, that they are recreated as innocent and are in some way also reconciled with God, might he not also have spoken of them as being justified? Perhaps his use of the term was not quite as theologically loaded or constrained as ours is. Perhaps it can apply to this strange creature caught between two worlds, one who is now innocent yet indelibly stained by sin.

Some exegetes have claimed that Paul always uses the term here translated "justification" as applying only to those who have trusted in Christ and are fully accepted by God, not anyone we might call unredeemably lost. But if some do exist in this state of being rejected by God and yet at peace with and in relationship with God, might Paul also speak of them as having "justification" or being "made alive"? If in every other case except Romans 5:18 it can be demonstrated that Paul's use of the term for justification applies *only* to those who are completely accepted by God, it is not inconceivable that he could also use the term here to include the lost who will love and be loved by God. Just because we are sticklers for absolute consistency does not mean that Paul must be. He might simply think, "Sure, I could use that term to include the lost as well as those who have trusted in Christ since in the end the lost will be in relationship with God anyway—even though they will not be saved."

If, as some biblical scholars believe, Romans 5:18 does not speak of all people being justified and alive in Christ but only a select group who trust in Jesus for salvation and are completely accepted by God, then the above discussion is unnecessary and may be ignored. In that case there will be some who will be unredeemably lost and the "all" in this passage who are justified and made alive does not include this category of people.

Jesus more than once taught that the lost will enter a place of punishment with a fire that will not be extinguished. Because he would say no more, it often sounded as though this would be the final unending state of the lost. But we have seen hints elsewhere in his teachings and even one or two fairly clear statements (if my analysis is correct) that would tell us that this is not their final end. We have even clearer statements throughout the Bible and especially throughout the rest of the NT that there is change to come after one's time of punishment. Jesus told his disciples that the Holy Spirit would give them more information later because they were not yet ready to receive it (John 16:12–13). Jesus was leaving it for others to more clearly tell the rest of the story:

They tell us that God will "reconcile to himself all things" and "bring unity to all things." "In Christ all will be made alive" to the final purpose "that God may be all in all." God is the "Savior of all people" and Jesus said "I will draw all people to myself." It seems clear that the way he had "mercy on . . . all" was by his act which "resulted in justification and life for all."[3] These are the final and deepest truths of Scripture. Jeremiah condensed the greatest of all promises when he said that "no one is cast off by the Lord forever" (Lam 3:31) and Isaiah restated it when he told us that God *cannot* forget us (any of us) and that God's love for all people is deeper than that of a mother for her newborn (Isa 49:15–16a). Though some will bear forever the shame of their rejection of God (Dan 12:2; Rev 14:11a), God's favor will last forever. For a moment God brings grief and destruction, but for eternity God will show compassion, "so great is his unfailing love" (Ps 30:5; Lam 3:32).

Much of the semi-restorationist view may appear very speculative. But speculation is entirely permissible where Scripture does not speak or where Scripture provides evidence for the speculation but does not speak with absolute certainty. The Bible does provide evidence for some of the points of semi-restorationism and it does not speak on other points. Speculation is especially appropriate when a speculative system can be constructed which answers extremely serious and troubling problems in theology. If semi-restorationism is not true, it at least shows that the problems can be potentially answered.

Nevertheless, I think I have given some good reasons to think it is true. If it is true it does justice, on the one hand, to Paul's promise that in the end all things will be reconciled to God (Col 1:20), while on the other, to his warning that those who reject God will endure destruction, cast out of God's presence (2 Thess 1:9). It takes into account the major problematic universalistic passages we have looked at. Such passages are indeed problematic for those who seek a consistent and coherent biblical theology which takes into account all of the relevant passages which bear on the subject. Without admitting to any form of forced salvation so common in

---

3. See the first heading under chapter 6 for more on these passages.

various forms of universalism, semi-restorationist still gives hope to those who have felt and known the anguish of the problem of lost loved ones. But it also gives hope to the lost. It give hope that all people will be given their highest good, the ultimate fulfillment of completeness and joy for which they were created: the ultimate good of knowing God.

8

OTHER FORMS OF INCLUSIVISM

We have considered what may be the initial and final condition of the lost after death and whether all of the lost are or are not unredeemably lost (figure 3). I have claimed that some may yet be offered salvation after a time of punishment (d2, figure 3). We have seen that there are no Scriptures which contradict this claim and that some support this possibility. I have also claimed that we cannot avoid the possibility that some are unredeemably lost at death (UL, figure 3). Our discussion of semi-restorationism applies to this group.

To fill out the picture, we now need to consider just what the Scripture tells us about whether there might be any others who will find complete redemption after death. Limited potential restorationism is a form of inclusivism, but might there be any other types? Specifically, might there be people whom God has judged to be as deserving as anyone else to hear and respond to the gospel before facing judgment but who have not had that ability or opportunity before death. A good case can be made for extending inclusivism to cover certain other categories of people.

John 7:17. "Anyone who chooses to do the will of God will find out whether my teaching comes from God or whether I speak on my own."

Acts 10:34–35. "Then Peter began to speak: 'I now realize how true it is that God does not show favoritism but accepts from every nation the one who fears him and does what is right.' "

Because here in Acts 10 it is said that God shows no favoritism and does not choose one person for salvation at the exclusion of any other, all people must be offered the opportunity to make the choices that will provide salvation. God would never keep any person from being able to choose. Yet to be saved one must accept God's gift of salvation by faith in Jesus Christ (Acts 4:12 above). Clearly, not everyone has the opportunity to hear of Jesus in this life in order to make this choice. Also, there are many people of different religions as well as nonreligious people who have heard of Christianity but who reject it because they have not understood its claims or evidence. It is possible that some have never seen anything other than a mere caricature of Christianity even though many of them have earnestly sought God and sought the truth from God. Some people have had such strongly negative experiences with professed Christians or with Christian authorities or institutions that they seem to be completely incapable of honestly considering the evidence for Christianity. God does sometimes give healing to people with such horrible incapacities; God can heal the most distorted, twisted minds. But I cannot claim that God always does so. So if I could state it paradoxically, I think there are many people who have heard of Christianity who have never heard of Christianity. That is, they are the same as those who have never heard of Christianity in their incapacity to respond to the Christian message.

I would resolve this problem as follows: First we should look at John 7:17. Jesus essentially says that those who will to do God's will shall know that Jesus' teachings are of God. So the decision that determines salvation is more basically seeking God and seeking the truth from God, willing to do God's will. With this, one will discover God's will in the truth of Christianity and, because one wills to do God's will, will trust in Jesus for salvation (A, figure 1). Other passages confirm this principle that the basic issue is to seek God, whether one believes God exists or not. They tell us that those who seek God will find and that those who merely call upon God will be saved (Jer 29:13; Rom 10:13; Joel 2:32; Acts 17:27). No one is ever ultimately lost or saved because of what they *know*; they are accepted or rejected by God because of what they *choose*.

John 7 does not make it clear that those who seek God and will to do God's will shall inevitably discover the truth of Christianity *in this life*. The possibility must be open that some may not discover this until after death, whether they have heard the gospel or not. Hebrews 9:27, discussed earlier, merely tells us that it is appointed to people to die once and then face judgment. It says nothing to preclude postmortem salvific decisions prior to judgment. So all people do have the opportunity to make the choice that will allow them to be accepted by God, though for some people, in this life at least, that decision may be no more than to seek God and to seek to do God's will. Nevertheless, sooner or later, whether before death or after, all must accept God's offer of salvation through Jesus Christ and trust in him for that salvation if they are to be accepted by God (A, d1', figure 5).

Secondly, we should look again at the revelation to Peter in Acts 10 above. Those who honor and reverence God and seek to do what is right, we are told, will be accepted by God (A, d1, figure 5). Again, however, they must profess faith in Christ (Acts 4:12 above). It necessarily follows that if such people have not heard the Christian message in this life, they will hear and believe in the next (A, d1', figure 5). It also follows that if there are some who have heard the Christian message in this life and have rejected it in this life and yet who do truly honor and reverence God and seek to do what is right, then they too will know that Christianity is true at or after death and will choose then (A, d1', figure 5). If they reject what God shows them after death and they know that this is from God, if they refuse to trust in Christ, this would show that they have no true reverence or fear of God and possibly never really did. It would show an unwillingness to obey what God now asks of them (at d1' for RL & UL, figure 4).

Don Richardson, in his book, *Eternity in their Hearts*, recounts how several known people groups in Africa and Asia had anticipated the coming of Christian missionaries.[1] They had become alienated from the creator God they once knew and served and loved. Their traditions kept alive their longing for God, their despair over being bound to demonic spirits, and the promise they were given that someday God would bring them back to a knowledge of how they could again find and know God. Some even had prophets and traditions which spoke of white skinned people who would come with a book to show them the way to God. For those living in Buddhist countries, recurrent Buddhist missionary efforts were fruitless to convert them. Those living among Hindus refused to adopt Hinduism. But when Christian missionaries came, thousands became followers of Jesus. Professed Christians came to constitute sometimes well over 80 percent of some populations.

Richardson provides too much evidence that God had indeed promised them that their descendants would in their earthly lives find reconciliation with God. In one instance one of their prophets told his followers that God had told him that the time had finally come. He told them to untie a donkey and let it go free. Some of his disciples were to follow the donkey for they were told that it would lead them to the man who would show them how to find God. The donkey walked about 200 miles until it came to a city and then walked to the home of one of the first Christian missionaries to this country.[2]

Can we imagine that these people who generation after generation, century after century, longed to find God should be thought of as eternally lost simply because they never in their lives heard the gospel? The promise cannot be only for those who eventually heard. Even if the promise was not fulfilled in their lifetimes, it must also include those who never heard but who longed to be

1. Richardson, *Eternity*, 50–55, 65–96.
2. Richardson, *Eternity*, 78, 91–93.

among those who would hear. It is unimaginable that God would say to a people, "I give this promise, this gift to you. This is how I show my love to you. Your people will be brought back to me someday. There is no gift more wonderful than this because this is the reason you were created. You yourselves, however, must remain eternally alienated from me."

Some people who have heard the Christian message lack the psychological ability to freely choose God in this life because of their past experiences. Many lack the ability to even seek God. God, who searches our hearts, knows who it is who has maliciously rejected God without good reason (RL & UL, figure 3) and who has been unwittingly caught in deception. Many of the latter will surely be included among those who are given another opportunity after death to accept God's offer of salvation (at d1' for RL & UL, figure 4). With no good scriptural grounds to disbelieve this, what we know from Scripture of God's absolute goodness, love, justice, and lack of favoritism (Acts 10:34) would surely require another opportunity for people like this. As Abraham said, "Will not the Judge of all the earth do right?" (Gen 18:25).

We should now look at some passages which some believe refute these claims.

Romans 10:9, 14. "If you declare with your mouth, 'Jesus is Lord,' and believe in your heart that God raised him from the dead, you will be saved. . . . How can they believe in the one of whom they have not heard? And how can they hear without someone preaching to them?"

This passage is often cited to claim that all must hear the gospel and respond to it in this life if they are to be accepted by God. But these verses say nothing about when it must be proclaimed to them, whether in this life or in the next. Moreover, Paul shortly says that all have heard (v. 18) and thus all have sufficient knowledge that their choices now will determine their salvation. Obviously all have not heard the explicit Christian message, so Paul must mean that the Holy Spirit calls to and draws all in this life (with some possible exceptions noted below) and that all who as a result seek God and will to do God's will or all who honor God and seek to do what is right will be accepted by God. God gives them enough information (they have "heard") that they must make the decisions to seek or honor God.

Those who respond positively to the Holy Spirit's drawing to seek and honor God (on sometimes nothing more than merely the possibility that God is there) will hear the explicit offer of salvation at or after death and they will respond according to their earlier choices (A, figure 5). Many who seek God in this way will hear the Christian message in this life. Many who have not heard the gospel in this life, if they respond negatively to the drawing of the Holy Spirit and to what they know by nature of God's existence and goodness (Rom 1:18–21), will have no future opportunity to respond again before enduring God's judgment (RL & UL, figure 3), though possibly some will be given that postmortem, pre-punishment opportunity (RL & UL, d₁', figure 4). However, many who respond negatively, if they must first face God's judgment may be given the opportunity to respond to the gospel after their time of punishment is over (limited potential restorationism, see RL, d₂, figure 3).

But does it follow that everyone without exception has "heard" in this life? Will all be either lost of saved only according to their choices in response to this general revelation and to the calling of God's Spirit or even in response to hearing the Christian message? As an obvious example of someone who has not heard (in this manner), we might think of those who have died too young to have heard the gospel. I think we can add to this group those who have never understood the gospel if they had heard it and those who have never yet had God's Spirit draw them or call them to God (B, figure 5). If Christians think about it carefully, they will also usually admit that there may be some who have mental deficiencies that disallow them the ability to respond to God. Paul cannot mean that absolutely everyone must make a decision in this life which will determine their salvation.

Paul's statement that all have heard must thus be taken as merely a general principle with possible exceptions. Like his statement that political authorities are only a danger to those who do evil, not those who do good (Rom 13:3), he knew very well that both the Jewish and Gentile rulers could be a danger to Christians who only do good. He knew that there was a legitimate place for disobeying such authorities (rebelling against them, v. 2), such as when they would order a believer to no longer proclaim the gospel (cf. Acts 5:29). We have looked at Hebrews 9 and seen that it likewise provides only a general principle that admits of exceptions.

I think we could add to the list of those who are mentally unable to respond to God or the gospel. For example, I've noted that there are many who have had such negative experiences with the church that they are incapable of hearing or responding to God. If these spiritual blockages are not removed before death, wouldn't God allow them to be removed after death so that they would be able to choose then?

Just one example to press my point: I know of someone who grew up in the American South and attended an all white "Christian" school for many of his early years. The students were spoon fed racism and hatred of blacks. One teacher joked, "I have nothing against n——s, I think everyone should own one." This man now cannot even consider commitment to Christ because his thinking so strongly associates Jesus with hatred and bigotry. It does no good to point out that Jesus' life and teaching were totally antithetical to such obscenities. The years of immersion in this mindset have bound him; he is unable to honestly evaluate and consider Christianity.

So it seems most likely that there are some whose salvation is not determined until after death but before any time of postmortem punishment. I've even suggested elsewhere that there may be some, like those who have died too young, whom God will allow to live another life either in another world much like our own or possibly even again in this world. We have seen that Hebrews 9:27 only states as a general principle that people will not live on earth more than once. It does not apply to the exceptions of those who have died too young.

We need to look at some other passages that are often cited to claim that any who hear the gospel and do not believe in this life are necessarily lost.

John 3:18. "Whoever believes in him is not condemned, but whoever does not believe stands condemned already because they have not believed in the name of God's one and only Son."

The apostle John (as I believe wrote or dictated this passage or something very much like it) here assumes that the unbeliever does clearly know that they have disbelieved in God's only Son. John must surely be correct; to knowingly disregard the truth would normally be deserving of God's judgment.

Those who choose to will to do God's will shall not be condemned even if initially they do not believe in Jesus. It sometimes takes time to become aware of the evidence or of God's leading to believe. One who knows it is true and wills to do God's will, will believe. Sometimes even here, however, psychological barriers must first be overcome—but they will be overcome eventually. It is the choice, what one wills not what one knows, that is crucial. One who wills to do God's will shall be given sufficient reason to believe, either in this life or after death. We will all be responsible for our ultimate choice.

Not all who hear the gospel are aware that what they hear is true. This passage applies only to those who do clearly know it is true and sufficiently understand it and, as we have just seen, even they are not always immediately responsible for rejecting it. Likewise, the justification or condemnation of those who do not know that it is true will depend upon their decision then or at a later time to will to do God's will.

John 8:24. "If you do not believe that I am he, you will indeed die in your sins."

These words may apply only to these particular listeners. These are very likely the same people who had previously witnessed notable miracles from Jesus. As the previous passage we have considered indicates, they had enough good evidence to believe so that they would be held accountable if they continued in disbelief. Normally, people would show that they have no fear of God and do not seek to will God's will if they reject what they know is true (RL & UL, figure 3).

Mark 16:16. "Whoever believes and is baptized will be saved, but whoever does not believe will be condemned."

This would be a powerful prooftext were it not for the fact that we do not know that Jesus really said it. This is from a portion of Mark that was not in the original text. It was added later. We simply cannot use this passage as a prooftext because it cannot be considered part of the inspired Scripture.

2 Thessalonians 2:12. "All will be condemned who have not believed the truth but have delighted in wickedness."

This passage emphasizes that one's condemnation follows from one's choice, one's choice to "[delight] . . . in wickedness" and (v. 10) "[refuse] . . . to love the truth." We are indeed lost or saved not by our knowledge but by our choices given the knowledge that we do have.

Act 13:46. "Then Paul and Barnabas answered them boldly: 'We had to speak the word of God to you first. Since you reject it and do not consider yourselves worthy of eternal life, we now turn to the Gentiles.' "

This certainly indicates that there may be some who will not have eternal life because they reject the gospel, but it is not clear that all will continue to reject it (see Rom 11:23). So even if my inclusivism is rejected, Barnabas and Paul's statement cannot be taken as saying that some will definitely be lost according to their present decision. If there were any among this group who rejected the gospel who willed to do God's will or who honored and reverenced God and sought to do what is right, then we are told in John 7 and Acts 10 that God would eventually lead them to accept it. Though it *may* be that God always leads such people to accept the truth of Christianity during their time on earth, we cannot know that this is so (A, figure 5). Exclusivism cannot be demonstrated to be true even though we must admit that no one can be accepted by God without faith in Jesus Christ. Only if they renounce their commitment to seek, reverence, and obey God might they be lost. Temptations such a social pressures may indeed influence people to reject their commitment to seek, obey, and commit themselves to God.

There is certainly no biblical principle or Scripture that tells us one must know of and profess faith in Christ in this life to be saved. If that were so, all of the Old Testament saints would be lost. And the Scripture is abundantly clear that that is not the case. To claim that they are saved but that everyone else who has not heard in this life is lost is just special pleading. Why should all who have lived after the time of Jesus need to hear of him and believe in him in their lifetimes to be saved but not those who lived before him? With this we should conclude that some will not be lost though they had never heard of Jesus during their lifetimes. But likewise, of those who had heard the Christian message, we have nothing in the Scripture that tells us that absolutely all must believe and be justified prior to death.

All Christians are obligated to influence as many people as possible to embrace Jesus as Lord and savior in this life. But for those who will not hear, we must seek to influence them to at least seek God, to seek the truth from God, and to seek to do God's will. Since there are many who will not do so, many of these will be held responsible for rejecting Christ in their lifetimes.

9

PRACTICAL CONSEQUENCES
FOR CHRISTIANITY

Universalists and eternalists have had a long history of squabbling over the practical consequences of the their own and their opponent's positions. Eternalists have claimed that people will not even consider Christianity if they thought universalism were true. Why make the moral sacrifices Christianity requires or be willing to lose all things, even one's life as Jesus taught, if all will be saved?

Restorationist universalism might say one should do so because the comparable cost of suffering in the next life will be very great for those who reject God even though they will eventually be saved. Certainly this does give some reason for embracing Christianity. Yet such a response seems to reduce the entire issue to a cold calculation of ultimate benefit vs. loss. The notion of embracing God's gift out of gratitude for the enormous sacrifice God has endured is a much more noble motive. When this reason is included, the restorationist does provide good motivation for accepting Christ, though this view still suffers from the biblical and philosophical problems considered earlier. Simple universalism (all go directly to heaven with no time of purgation or punishment in between), on the other hand, provides far less reason for one to consider Christianity. This claim is substantiated as we see history strewn with so many universalist churches and movements that have wasted away or even vanished from the face of the earth.

Universalists have similarly claimed that eternalism has kept many non-Christians from considering Christianity and many Christians from continuing to adhere to their faith. For example, I began this study talking about James Mill's refusal to consider an eternalist Christianity. The doctrine of an eternal hell was a major reason Bertrand Russell opposed Christianity. It was one of the problematic doctrines that began to chip away at Charles Darwin's early evangelical faith. It was difficult for him to accept that so many close relatives and friends would be spending eternity in agonizing torment. Most of us can think of people we know who say that this doctrine has had much to do with their rejection of Christianity.

I remember visiting a very fundamentalist Baptist Church years ago. They were holding a special "evangelistic" event utilizing a movie about the horrors of hell. The movie dwelt on points that would bring home to the common people how extremely painful it would be to be in hell and how very long "forever" is. One illustration, as accurately as I can remember, was of a bird taking a grain of sand or soil from the earth, taking a million years to fly to the moon, depositing that grain on the moon, flying back to the earth for another grain (another million years—and the same for every flight), and eventually removing every bit of earth to the moon one grain at a time. With this unimaginably long time we were told "eternity has not even begun" and the excruciating agony of those in hell will be just as great after this time as it was when it started.

People did "come to the alter" for salvation, some (mostly children) with profuse weeping and great fear. Some of these people may have remained Christians over the years, but I wonder how many. Once a person is able to think through their beliefs and the reasons they believe, if they have nothing more than an experience like this to ground their faith, they will more likely fall away. How many other people at this event did not run to the alter but walked away only to reject Christianity entirely because of this movie?

So the question of who has done the most harm for the propagation of the cause of Christ remains open, eternalism or simple universalism. Though restorationist universalism does fare better, I think semi-restorationism would do best of all.

The problem of lost loved ones is resolved by universalism and semi-restorationism but remains a difficulty for annihilationists and, even more so, for eternalists. Consider the problem from merely the view of the redeemed. It is hardly satisfying to accept the possibility that in heaven God will erase from our minds the memories of the annihilated or suffering damned. Possibly worse is the prospect that God stoically accepts the eternal suffering or annihilation of the lost and the redeemed will come to learn to conform their minds to God's mind. Definitely worse is the prospect that God rejoices that justice is done and we must learn to do so as well. The God of the Bible does not rejoice in the death or punishment of the lost (Ezek 33:11). God is not willing that any should perish (Matt 18:14; 2 Pet 3:9). If the saints in paradise will never remember their lost loved ones, it is still very devastating to *now* know that they will be eternally gone or, worse, suffer eternal agony.

The other forms of inclusivism discussed in this study will also have practical consequences. If Christians admit that after death there are opportunities to respond to God's offer of salvation for some who were not able to before, then Christianity will not be seen as the unjust belief exclusivism paints it to be.[1] The practical consequences of these different views are far reaching and will affect how people respond to Christianity.

---

1. Some additional reflection on exclusivism given Molinism and the inherited sin nature can be found in the commentary section for figure 1 in the appendix.

CONCLUSION

Semi-restorationism lacks the moral and philosophical deficiencies found in other Christian positions. It lacks what seems to many to be an almost belligerent tone in some forms of eternalism. (Historically, some eternalists have even maintained that it is part of the joy of the redeemed to eternally witness the agonies of the damned!) Semi-restorationism lacks universalism's disregard for the dignity of human free choice. It also lacks simple Christian universalism's sometimes complete disregard for the enormity of Jesus' sacrifice. Under semi-restorationism, non-Christians may be warned of the enormous suffering and loss that will result from their knowingly rejecting God's great sacrifice or of their willful disregard of their obligation to seek God (John 3:18; 7:17; Isa 55:3a). Yet they can be assured that God will be just and that in some way, in the end, all things will be reconciled to God and the greatest possible good will be done given the choices they had made.

Nevertheless, they should also be warned that semi-restorationism is not absolutely certain and that on the possibility that Christian annihilationism is true, one should not put one's hope in a future which may not come to be. Unlike simple universalism, semi-restorationism hardly offers a pleasant prospect for those who reject God. Just punishment, however limited in time, will occur. It offers hope for those who reject God but only through a hard and painful process. Yet the annihilationist future is much more frightening. Just punishment *and* annihilation may be the rightful end of those who reject God. No, it's not *that much* different from secular annihilationism, but whoever thought secular annihilationism to be anything less than frightening?

God had allowed intense pain to come upon Job. In his agony, Job complained bitterly. He wondered at how this could be. In Job 10 he questions God:

> "You gave me life and showed me kindness,
>   and in your providence watched over my spirit. . . .
> Your hands shaped me and made me.
>   Will you now turn and destroy me? . . .
> Did you not . . . clothe me with skin and flesh
>   and knit me together with bones and sinews? . . .
> Does it [now] please you to oppress me,
>   to spurn the work of your hands . . . ?"
>   (vv. 12, 8, 10, 11, 3)

Job did not know that God had special reason for allowing the suffering that he had to endure, just as God has reason for all who endure such pain (see Job 1–2). But Job did know that if God had no such reason then this is simply not something one should expect of our creator; indeed, it would indict his God as being evil.

The notion that the source and creator of all existence could curse any sentient creation with eternal pain and torment just does not fit what we know our God must be like. A good God would not allow one even the opportunity or ability to make a choice that would deserve such pain. Job is saying that he cannot conceive of how God could allow even a much milder suffering if it has no good reason and cannot be redeemed. With this very obvious intuition, we know that something must be wrong with the traditional view, with any claim that the Bible teaches eternal, horrific suffering and pain for some. Our examination of the most important biblical passages shows that eternalism is not true.

We were created from God's very own being, from God's Spirit-Breath. Our source and creator will not ultimately harm us.

Our ultimate end will be our good. Job's words are the same words everyone must speak, from the most righteous to the most wicked. God did not create even the most evil person to endure suffering forever. Job understood that the God who watched over our spirits and showed us kindness as we grew and lived could not do that.

I said earlier that it is not inconceivable that God could choose to create us and then annihilate us. Though Job probably understood death to involve annihilation, he may have had some glimpse of there being more of life to come after death. In this passage we see one of those hints that the God he loved was the kind of God who would not create us just to destroy us. Though it would be entirely within God's rights to annihilate any of us, whether wicked of righteous, and we could imagine God creating us as intrinsically temporally finite creatures, we see here a deeper awareness in Job. The God Job knew would not do that.

Those who accept annihilationism should be commended: annihilationism is at least more likely than eternalism. I should mention that one of the greatest deficiencies of secular annihilationism, belief in extinction at death, is that justice is never carried out. Hitler or Stalin never receive justice for the horrible evils they had done. Christian annihilationism remedies this.

Nevertheless, I must insist that the better answer is not Christian annihilationism but semi-restorationism. Annihilationism takes all hope from those who have lost loved ones. I have argued that the God described in the Bible is above all else a God of love who will not do this. Neither is the better answer universalism which ultimately disregards human freedom. Universalism denies that, with the grace of God which is given to all people, we can choose to accept or reject God's gift and to make ourselves into something good and beautiful or something hideous and evil and deserving of God's judgment. It denies that something of that self-creation will be permanent. Neither is the better answer eternalism which destroys all hope for the lost and creates a world of misery unworthy of God, a hideous tumor of unending sin and agony and hatred at the core of God's perfect and beautiful final creation. The better answer is semi-restorationism which allows the lost just punishment and loss but also allows for a restoration to life and joy. This joy is not as great as it could be had they not rejected God, but it is greater than anything experienced in this life. It offers hope that any other Christian view other than universalism cannot give.

We have seen that though there will be many whose decisions in this life will determine whether or not they face God's judgment and punishment in the next life, there will be others whose salvific decisions will wait until after death. Some of those who, according to their decisions, must bear the punishment their sins deserve, may yet be offered a final opportunity to find reconciliation with God. There may be some who endure their punishment and are offered no further opportunity for salvation. All depends upon what decisions were made and the character of those decisions. The God who searches the depths of our hearts knows who has made their choices with sufficient information and understanding and who has not. The Judge of all the earth will be just.

God does all that can be done to call humanity back to God. But after we have all made our choices and some have finally and completely rejected their God, and after they have endured all of the punishment justice requires of them, God will again have mercy. God will not allow them the full joy and good they could have had had they not rejected God, but they will be given their portion of the greatest of all joys, the joy of knowing God. All will find the fulfillment and joy for which we were created.

Oral Roberts had a son who died as an unbeliever. The parents lived with the horrible fear that their son was and would eternally be suffering the agonies of hell. They cried out to God and in their anguish God led them to a passage of Scripture. "Perfect love drives out fear," John wrote in his epistle. They felt that God was telling them that whatever they believed about the afterlife of the lost, they would have hope and they must not fear. They knew that God would not allow their worst fears to be realized.

Perhaps the unbelieving son is among those who will be given another chance to trust in Christ after their time of punishment is over (limited potential restorationism). Perhaps he is among those who, at death, are allowed another chance to choose (inclusivism). It may be that he can never be redeemed and someday after much suffering he will be reunited with his parents in the communion of God's love (semi-restorationism). But then again, it may be that God has another plan for his deliverance that is far different from anything we might imagination.

However God does it, God will wipe away all of the parents' tears—as God will wipe away our tears as well.

I began this study saying that Christians must demonstrate that the God described in the Bible would be absolutely good, loving, and just. I have begun to do this by noting some of the scriptural passages which describe God's goodness, love, and justice as well as by demonstrating that some passages which might imply lack of love, goodness, and justice do not do so. God's love has been primarily demonstrated by the incarnation and atonement. Assuming the biblical teachings concerning the human condition, God endured great suffering to bring us back to God and to fully free us from the judgment our sins would otherwise require, if we would but accept it.

I have only dealt with a select group of those passages which might imply lack of goodness, justice, or love: those which suggest eternal suffering for some in an afterlife. I have not dealt explicitly with other passages such as God's command to the Israelites to exterminate large groups of people or God's act of destroying most of humanity in the great Flood. Of course, the problem of an eternal hell is an enormously greater problem. Other studies have dealt with these other problems and one must look there for better, more complete answers.[1] Nevertheless, I think we have gone over certain principles which provide the most basic answers to some of these other problems. We have seen that God has the right to take any human life at any time God wishes. We have also seen that God has the right to judge people who do evil and that God will be just.

1. As a good introduction to such problems, see Copan, *Moral Monster*.

But all in all, we have reached our goal. By resolving the problem of an eternal hell, we see that in this particular area of scriptural teaching the God of the Bible is absolutely good, just, and loving.

Appendix

FIGURES AND ANNOTATION

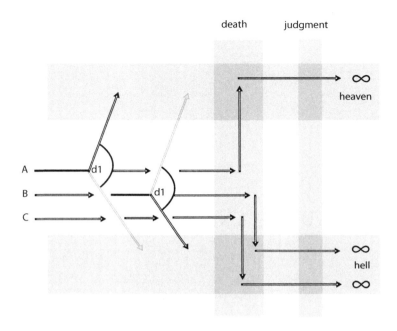

Figure 1. Exclusivism, Eternalism (Traditionalism)

A, B, and C are three representative individuals.

Under exclusivism, those (A) who have heard the Christian message and choose to repent of their sin and believe in Jesus (d1) will be saved while those (B) who do not so choose (d1) will be lost. Each person must in this life choose to accept or reject God by accepting or rejecting God's offer of salvation through Christ. Those (C) who have no opportunity to choose in this life, such as those who have not heard the offer of salvation, are normally considered lost. Under eternalism, those who are lost are lost forever and they endure suffering forever.

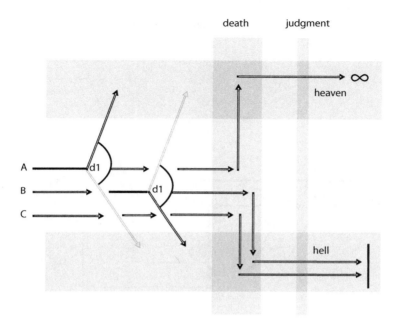

Figure 2. Annihilationism (Conditional Immortality)

The most obvious difference between eternalism and annihilationism is that annihilationism says the consciousness of the lost will be exterminated after a time of suffering in hell. Exclusivism is assumed in this diagram. (See commentary.)

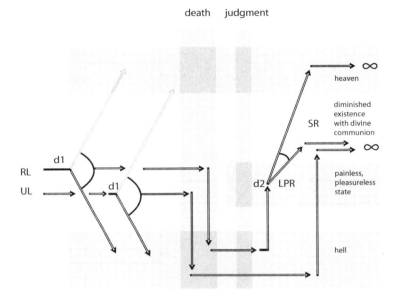

Figure 3. Semi-restorationism with Limited Potential Restorationism (Inclusivism 1).

RL: redeemably lost, no postmortem opportunity to accept salvation before time of punishment, but an opportunity after.

UL: unredeemably lost, no postmortem opportunity to accept salvation before time of punishment and no opportunity after. Pre-mortem decisions (d1) determine whether they are RL or UL.

RL's and UL's decision at d1 may be pre-mortem choices in response to the gospel or choices in response to God's universal calling without knowledge of the gospel.

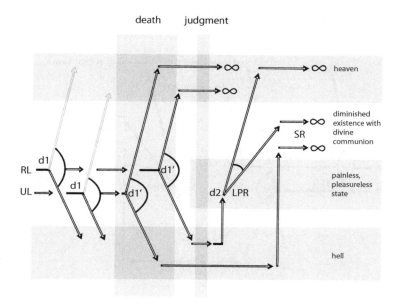

death judgment

Figure 4. Semi-restorationism with Limited Potential Restorationism (Inclusivism 1). Additional Opportunity at Death for Salvific Decision (Inclusivism 2).

RL: redeemably lost, second opportunity to accept salvation before time of punishment (d1') and third opportunity after (at d2).

UL: unredeemably lost, second opportunity before time of punishment but no opportunity after. Their decisions at d1' as well as their pre-mortem decisions determine whether they are RL or UL.

Since we accept that God's judgments will be just and right according to the choices we make, we should assume that under some conditions God will allow the RL and UL another opportunity at or after death (d1'). Because it may be that some of the UL are not such until a final decision is offered at death (d1'), we leave open as a possibility that God does sometimes allow this opportunity. RL and UL's decision at d1 may be pre-mortem choices in response to the gospel or choices in response to God's universal calling without knowledge of the gospel.

APPENDIX

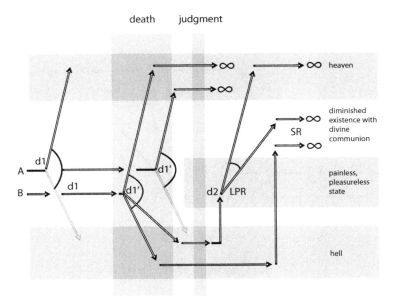

Figure 5. Inclusivism 3

Group A. Those who have responded positively to God's general revelation and universal calling at d1 and will respond positively to the knowledge of the gospel when given at d1'.

Group B. Those who have not received God's universal calling and will be given opportunity to respond to the gospel after death (d1').

KEY

Arrows. The path of several arrows is continuous only when one arrow points to the origin point of another arrow or line or the origin point of two or three arrows that form an angle symbol. If the head of one arrow points to the side of a second arrow, it does not follow that second arrow but rather the starting end of the arrow or line directly ahead of it. For example, the arrow following B in figures 1 and 2 points to the side of a decision arrow for A; the arrow following B should rather follow the line directly ahead of it to the angle symbol at B's d1. Then it should continue following its original direction on the arrow connected to and continuing on to the right of the central curve of the angle sign. That arrow then connects to the descending arrow it points to. When an arrow leads to an angle symbol with two dark arrows, follow both dark arrows since this indicates that either alternative may be chosen and the path of the individual's continuing state corresponds with one of those arrows.

Angle symbol. The intersecting arrows with angle signs represent a point of decision. They are noted as d1, d1', or d2. The grayed arrow indicates that the decision was made negatively in that direction and positively in the direction of the darker arrow. The grayed arrow pointing in the direction of heaven and the darker arrows pointing downward would mean that God's offer of salvation is rejected. The darker arrow pointing upward and the grayed arrow pointing downward indicate a choice in the direction of God's offer of salvation.

Painless Pleasureless State. In figures 3, 4, and 5, this is a temporary state in which the redeemably lost will choose to accept or reject God and God's offer of reconciliation. This would be the final, eternal state of all of the lost who finally and irrevocably reject God if modified eternalism alone were true. For such individuals, all memories which could give pleasure or pain are removed and one's ability to freely choose to do evil would be eliminated.

LPR. Limited potential restorationism in figures 3 and 4 is indicated by RL being able to choose salvation after their time of punishment in hell is ended (d2). It is limited in that it does not apply to all of the lost (specifically, UL) and it is potential in that one is free to choose redemption or reject it. In figure 5, those in group B who reject God at d1' may or may not have opportunity to choose again at d2.

SR. Semi-restorationism in figures 3, and 4 is indicated as the final state of diminished existence with divine communion for both the UL and the RL who ultimately reject God's offer of redemption. They ultimately choose against God but will end in a state of communion with God and the saints and they will lack free will and most past memories. Also they will eternally be marked with the stigma of having rejected their God and creator. In figure 5, those in group B who reject God at d1' and d2, or in some cases at d1' only, will end here.

COMMENTARY

Figure 1, Exclusivism, Eternalism (Traditionalism)

The diagrams in this appendix are included to help visualize the several possible positions described in this book. Though I have in the Key a detailed explanation of the meaning and function of the several parts of the diagrams, each figure is intuitively fairly self-explanatory.

Exclusivists are not necessarily eternalists. Some of the unredeemably lost (UL) in figure 3 under semi-restorationism might be thought to fit an exclusivist but non-eternalist model so long as their decision at d1 is in response to the gospel and not in response to the drawing of the Holy Spirit without the knowledge of the gospel. Some eternalists could be inclusivists and hold that there may be a second opportunity at death for some of the lost to accept salvation but that those who at that point reject God will endure eternal suffering.

Some exclusivist eternalists believe that those who die too young to have heard or understood the gospel will not necessarily be lost, though there is difference of opinion as to what their fate will be. And of course, some believe that since those who have not heard have inherited a sin nature, they are necessarily damned. Some may try to mitigate this horrendous belief by saying that God foreknew that they would reject the gospel anyway if they had lived to hear it. (Some theologians have had the sense to see how harsh this sounds when applied to a stillborn fetus; nevertheless, they have still maintained this to be true of adults who have not heard the gospel. One would think they should see that it is no less harsh to say this of adults.) Whether speaking of infants or adults, this approach hardly eases the difficulty, even though the problem is intuitively easier to see when thinking of the very young. Imagine that an aborted fetus, if it is given a soul, without having even a moment's awareness of human life, should know of no existence other than eternal agony and torment. Yet this is the logical conclusion of exclusivistic eternalism which holds individuals responsible because of their sin nature or because of what God foreknew they would choose, unless (inconsistently) they are allowed special exemption because of their age.

Under exclusivism, the OT saints living before the time of Christ, those depicted as righteous in the Hebrew scriptures, are also usually accepted as saved though they had never heard of Jesus. Of course, again, it is difficult to understand how such a claim is not special pleading. Opinions vary as to the status of pre-Christian righteous Gentiles, though the unrighteous Jews and Gentiles are usually considered lost.

Much will of necessity go unmentioned in a diagram such as this and the others that follow. The resurrection could generally be added between death and judgment though this would not apply to all people since there will be some living when the resurrection occurs. The place of the moral life and its affect upon one's salvation will differ with the theologies of those who hold to exclusivism as well as the other positions considered in this study.

For example, as strongly as one may affirm *sola fides*, the belief that salvation is by faith alone, I know of no Protestant who believes that, say, a mafia hit-man can make a profession of faith in Christ and continue in his old life style and yet be accepted by God. This is also very easy to demonstrate biblically. Thus the above diagram should not be taken to indicate that for individual A, the decision for Christ is alone sufficient for salvation and that moral or life style factors have no relevance.

As another example, in the above diagram the Roman Catholic doctrine of purgatory would require a place of suffering for some Christians for a limited period of time before they enter heaven. The Christian's moral life will affect whether one enters purgatory or goes directly to heaven at death. The doctrine of purgatory is very similar to that of limited potential restorationism for the redeemably lost (RL) in figure 3 though there are also significant differences.

Figure 2, Annihilationism, (Conditional Immortality)

Depending on the type of annihilationism being considered, those in group C may or may not be lost. We could imagine several different variations of annihilationism. Some might allow for a second opportunity to accept salvation at or after death but before experiencing hell (as with RL or UL at d_1' in figure 4), and some might allow additionally an opportunity for reconciliation with God after a period of penal suffering (as in the limited potential restorationist position, LPR, at d_2 for the RL in figures 3 and 4). If semi-restorationism is not true, those who refuse at both or the last relevant possible point(s) of decision will be extinguished rather than enter a state of diminished existence and communion with God. Salvific decisions at d_1 for A and B are in response to clear knowledge of the gospel. In this diagram exclusivism is assumed and because C makes no salvific decision in response to the gospel or because C has no knowledge of the gospel, C is lost.

Figure 5, Inclusivism 3

Some additional forms of inclusivism are advocated in this study other than those mentioned in figures 3 and 4. (Those previously mentioned are limited potential restorationism, in which the redeemably lost, RL, are given a second choice at d2 in figure 3, also marked LPR at this point; and the possibility of a salvific opportunity at or soon after death for the redeemably lost, RL, and the unredeemably lost, UL, in figure 4 at each d1'.)

This diagram depicts a semi-restorationist view of the final state of the lost. The types of inclusivism discussed here could also fit the eternalist or annihilationist views. For example, under eternalism or annihilationism, if those in B at d1' choose to reject God, they will (respectively) either endure hell forever or be annihilated. If, given semi-restorationism, they leave hell after a limited period of suffering, it will be to enter the state marked as SR or to have a second opportunity to choose to enter heaven. The choice must be free, thus there cannot be any sense that one would be returning to a painful state if one chooses against God. If choosing God is perceived as more desirable, it must be primarily in the sense that one is aware that this is the right thing to do. Thus rejecting God may be seen as more desirable to some.

Group A constitutes a special group of those both before and after the time of Christ who have never heard the Christian message during their life times. These would be those who, during their life times, will have made positive decisions which would determine their salvations on the basis of God's calling and drawing of all people (Rom 10:13–14, 18). (There are some exceptions to this universal calling noted below.) Though they had believed (d1) with sufficient understanding of what God had revealed through nature in order to be accepted by God and they had fulfilled the basic requirement of seeking and honoring God (Rom 1:20; Jer 29:13; Acts 10:35; 17:27) to be accepted by God, they must (and will) still make an explicit decision for Christ at or after death (d1') when this information is revealed to them (John 7:17). Thus those of group A are described as positively choosing God both at d1 and d1'.

It is not difficult to conceive that some who have not heard the gospel will have chosen so strongly against God's drawing and against what God has revealed of God's existence, nature, and the moral law (Rom 1:18–21) that they will not be given another opportunity at death (d1') and will more appropriately be counted among the redeemably lost (RL) in figure 3, and possibly even among the unredeemably lost (UL) in figure 3.

Those who have never heard the gospel and who have rejected God's natural revelation but whom God has seen to have lacked sufficient knowledge to make a fully salvific decision will surely be given more information at or after death to make their decision at that time. They would be among those in B. It is also possible that God has other reasons for allowing this postmortem opportunity to some of those who have previously chosen against God's universal calling, though we might think of this group as more accurately being among the RL or UL in figure 4. Among the same group would be some who are only partially aware of God's universal calling who have rejected God. Since it seems pretty obvious that there are many people who are not aware of God's universal calling (see the following paragraph) there would also likely be some who are only partially aware of it.

Group B would also include those who have died too young to have heard or understood the gospel or even to have heard God's universal calling through the Holy Spirit. It will also include many who have certain mental handicaps as well as anyone else who has had no opportunity to respond in any way to God's calling before death. It possibly even includes some who have had such negative experiences of Christianity as to be unable to honestly consider it. Those in B will be either people who have never made any salvific decisions prior to death or those who have made decisions that God would not consider binding. Depending upon how clearly aware the latter were of the decisions they were making when they rejected Christianity and how responsible their decisions were, those who have had very negative experiences of Christianity will be included among B or among the redeemably lost (RL) or the unredeemably lost (UL) of figures 3 and 4. So even if God judges that some were sufficiently responsible in making their negative decision before death, depending upon the character of their decisions, it may be that God will yet allow them to be counted among even the RL in figure 4 and be given additional opportunities to choose.

Anyone who has not experienced the drawing of God's Spirit and become aware of what God asks of them must at some time do so and they must eventually explicitly accept God's means of salvation through Jesus to be accepted by God. Many, like those who have died very young, will have had no such experiences before death and may require much more than a very short amount of time to make a decision after death at d_1'. As the diagram indicates, those of group B, if they reject God's offer of salvation at d_1' may or may not be given another opportunity to accept God's offer of salvation after their time of suffering in hell is over. Much must surely depend upon how adamantly and repeatedly those in B have rejected God in d_1'. Notice the three pronged arrow at d_1' for group B. Their decision will determine whether they will be accepted by God, be redeemably lost, or be unredeemably lost.

In figures 3 and 4, d_1 may be pre-mortem choices in response to the gospel or choices in response to God's universal calling without knowledge of the gospel. Pre-mortem choices in figures 1 and 2 do assume only a decision in response to the gospel. Those in figure 5 are in either group A, having no knowledge of the gospel but only of God's calling, or they are in B and have no awareness of either, or they are in B and make decisions in response to the gospel or to God's universal calling alone but God does not consider these decisions binding.

SELECTIVE BIBLIOGRAPHY

Abbott, Edwin A. *Flatland: A Romance of Many Dimensions*. 6th ed. New York: Dover, 1952.

Anselm. *Cur Deus Homo*. 1098. In *Anselm: Basic Writings*. Edited and translated by Thomas Williams. Indianapolis: Hackett, 2007.

Augustine. *City of God*. Edited by David Knowles. Toronto: Penguin, 1972.

Balz, Horst. *Exegetical Dictionary of the New Testament*. Vol. 1. Edited by Horst Balz and Gerhard Schneider. Grand Rapids: Eerdmans, 1990. 46–48.

Bell, Rob. *Love Wins: A Book about Heaven, Hell, and the Fate of Every Person Who Ever Lived*. New York: HarperCollins, 2011.

Blomberg, Craig. *Historical Reliability of the Gospels*. 2nd ed. Downers Grove, IL: Inter Varsity, 2007.

Brower, Kent, and Mark Elliot, eds. *Eschatology in Bible and Theology: Evangelical Essays at the Dawn of a New Millenium*. Downers Grove, IL: Inter Varsity, 1999.

Bruce, F. F. *The New Testament Documents: Are they Reliable?* 5th ed. Downers Grove, IL: Inter Varsity, 1960.

Copan, Paul. *Is God a Moral Monster? Making Sense of the Old Testament God*. Grand Rapids: Baker, 2011.

Craig, William Lane. "Objections to the Ontological Argument." Interview with Kevin Harris. Reasonable Faith Podcast. *Reasonable Faith Website*, April 18, 2013. http://www.reasonablefaith.org/Objections-to-the-Ontological-Argument.

———. *Reasonable Faith*. 3rd ed. Wheaton, IL: Crossway, 2008.

Craig, William Lane vs. John Shelby Spong. "The Great Resurrection Debate." South Bend, IN: Bethel College, March 20, 2005. http://www.reasonablefaith.org/media/craig-vs-spong-bethel-college-indiana.

Crockett, William, ed. *Four Views on Hell*. Grand Rapids: Zondervan, 1996.

Fudge, E. W. *The Fire That Consumes: The Biblical Case for Conditional Immortality*. 2nd ed. Carlisle, UK: Paternoster, 1994.

Selective Bibliography

Gregg, Steve. *All You Want to Know about Hell: Three Christian Views of God's Final Solution to the Problem of Sin*. New York: HarperCollins, 2013.

Habermas, Gary R., and Michael Licona. *The Case for the Resurrection of Jesus.* Grand Rapids: Kregel, 2004.

Hilborn, David, ed. *The Nature of Hell: A Report by the Evangelical Alliance Commission on Unity and Truth among Evangelicals ACUTE.* Carlisle, UK: Paternoster, 2000.

Instone-Brewer, David. *The Jesus Scandals: Why He Shocked His Contemporaries (and Still Shocks Today)*. Grand Rapids: Monarch, 2012.

Keener, Craig. *The IVP Bible Background Commentary: New Testament.* Downers Grove, IL: Inter Varsity, 1993.

Klassen, Randy. *What Does the Bible Really Say about Hell? Wrestling with the Traditional View.* Telford, PA: Pandora, 2001.

Kronen, John, and Eric Reitan. *God's Final Victory: A Comprehensive Philosophical Case for Universalism.* New York: Continuum, 2011.

Kvanvig, Jonathan L. *The Problem of Hell.* New York: Oxford University Press, 1993.

Lewis. C. S. *The Great Divorce.* New York: MacMillan, 1946.

———. *The Last Battle.* New York: MacMillan, 1944.

———. *The Problem of Pain.* New York: MacMillan, 1944.

Mill, John Stuart. *Autobiography.* 1873. Published from the original manuscript in the Columbia University Library with a preface by John Jacob Coss. New York: Columbia University Press, 1924.

Moo, Douglas. *The Wycliffe Exegetical Commentary: Romans 1–8.* Edited by Kenneth Barker. Chicago: Moody, 1991.

Munsch, Robert. *Love You Forever.* Willowdale, Ontario: Firefly, 1987.

Parry, Robin [Gregory MacDonald, pseud.]. *The Evangelical Universalist.* 2nd ed. Eugene, OR: Wipf & Stock, 2012.

Parry, Robin, and Christopher Partridge, eds. *Universal Salvation? The Current Debate.* Grand Rapids: Eerdmans, 2003.

Pinnock, Clark H., and R. C. Brow. *Unbounded Love: A Good News Theology for the 21st Century.* Downers Grove, IL: Inter Varsity, 1994.

Powys, D. J. *Hell–A Hard Look at a Hard Question: The Fate of the Unrighteous in New Testament Thought.* Carlisle, UK: Paternoster, 1998.

Preuss, H. D. *Theological Dictionary of the Old Testament.* Vol. 10. Edited by G. Johannes Botterweck, et al. Translated by Douglas W Scott. Grand Rapids: Eerdmans, 1999. 530–45.

Ramelli, Ilaria, and David Konstan. *Terms for Eternity: Aiônios and Aïdios in Classical and Christian Texts.* Piscataway, NJ: Gorgias, 2011.

Richardson, Don. *Eternity in their Hearts.* 3rd ed. Ventura, CA: Regal, 2005.

Sasse, Hermann. *Theological Dictionary of the New Testament.* Vol. 1. Edited by Gerhard Kittel and Gerhard Friedrich. Translated by Geoffrey W. Bromiley. Grand Rapids: Eerdmans, 1964. 208–9.

Sterba, James, ed. *God? A Debate Between a Christian and an Atheist.* New York: Oxford University Press, 2004.

Talbott, Thomas. *The Inescapable Love of God.* Rev. ed. Parkland: Universal, 2002.

Till, Eric, director. "A Simple Reply." *Luther.* DVD. Beverly Hills, CA: Metro Goldwyn Mayer, 2003.

Walls, J. *Hell: The Logic of Damnation.* Notre Dame: University of Notre Dame Press, 1992.

Wenham, John. *Facing Hell: The Story of a Nobody.* Carlisle, UK: Paternoster, 1998.

Wright, N. T. *Jesus and the Victory of God.* Christian Origins and the Question of God 2. London: SPCK, 1996.

———. *The Resurrection of the Son of God.* Christian Origins and the Question of God 3. Minneapolis: Fortress, 2003.

CPSIA information can be obtained at www.ICGtesting.com
Printed in the USA
LVOW01s1814140714

394272LV00036B/2102/P